THE POSTMAN

Roger Martin du Gard

THE POSTMAN

Translated by
JOHN RUSSELL

HOWARD FERTIG

NEW YORK · 1975

Originally published in France as *Vieille France*
Copyright 1933 by Librairie Gallimard, Paris
Copyright 1955 by The Viking Press, Inc.
Howard Fertig, Inc. Edition 1975
Published by arrangement with The Viking Press, Inc.

Library of Congress Cataloging in Publication Data
Martin du Gard, Roger, 1881-1958.
     The postman.
     Translation of Vieille France.
     Reprint of the ed. published by Viking Press, New
York.
     I.   Title.
PZ3.M3665Po6   [PQ2625.A823]   843'.9'12
74-13052

Printed in the United States of America

To Christiane and to Marcel de Coppet,
this simple album of village sketches.

R.M.G.

1

Joigneau struck a match.

La Mélie turned irritably towards the wall.

'What time is it?'

'Quarter past.'

He groaned, got out of bed, and pushed the shutters open. The sun was up: less of a lie-a-bed, in late July, than the village postman. The sky was pink; pink, too, were the sleeping houses, and pink the dust in the deserted square, where the trees laid long shadows, as they did in the evening.

Joigneau put on his trousers and went out into the courtyard to make water. He was a great hairy giant of a man: wind and dust and sun had bleached the red from his hair and turned his complexion to copper.

In three minutes he was ready: dressed, from képi to gaiters, for the rest of the day.

La Mélie slept in a light chemise during the hot weather. One plump shoulder came up above the sheet:

'Not so much noise – you'll wake Joseph.'

The wheelwright's apprentice slept upstairs, in the attic which would otherwise have served no purpose, since the postman had no children.

Joigneau didn't answer. Much he cared if he woke up the boy! And the boy didn't care either: he was already about, with his shirt on: barefoot, his ears pricked.

As soon as he heard the postman go out he slipped down like a monkey to the threshold of the bedroom below:

'Madame Joigneau – what's the time?'

She was waiting for him. Uneasily, with her breath coming fast and her eyes on the unbolted door, she replied:

'Nearly half-past.'

If the door had been made of glass she could not have seen him more clearly as he stood there, with one hand scratching his untidy head, his shirt un-buttoned across his chicken-white breast, his eyes blinking and his big lips half open.

A moment's silence, and then:

'Right you are,' he said. He stayed a minute longer – listening, as La Mélie was listening, to the silence. Then – the idiot! – he was back upstairs in three great bounds, with his shirt-tail flying in the air.

Madame Joigneau heard him close his door and hurl himself on his bed. She gave a sigh, arched her back, and yawned. Then she got up, bolted the door and began her toilet.

*   *   *

The post office of Maupeyrou is only five minutes from the station; but the station – because of the uphill stretch of the Bois-Laurent – is a good quarter of an hour from the post office.

Joigneau moved noiselessly between the silent house-fronts, with his delivery-bag on his shoulder.

The village was long and narrow, with no streets other than the road which ran straight through it and grudgingly grew wide enough, in the centre of the village, to encircle the church. At that hour, Maupeyrou was still asleep. One of the earliest risers was Bosse, who owned the café in the square; but he'd not yet opened his shutters. Even the bakery was shut. They took life easily, those bakers: two old bachelors, Merlavigne by name, who took it in turn to sit up all night at the oven. At this moment in the early morning, however, they were both at leisure; the one had finished making the bread, and the other had not yet begun to sell it.

Féju, on the other hand, was always up early. He was already chopping logs in front of his woodshed before leaving for work.

'Morning, Féju,' Joigneau called out.

The roadmender, bent nearly double, replied with a nod of the head. His back was always bent, as if under a sack of flour. An extraordinary fellow, Féju: the year before, he'd vanished for seventeen days. Seventeen days, and not a trace of him. The police had had to take a hand. He'd been marked as 'missing' on the strength of the county council. And then, one fine morning, he'd been back as usual, in the middle of the road, with his head bent over the stones, his bicycle in the ditch, and his lunch in the cool of the grass. And nobody had ever got to know what had really happened – not even Joigneau. Had he been on the loose with a pretty woman from Villegrande? Or had he gone off by himself? Had he just taken it into his head to disappear? To go off and leave them all flat – his four children, his sick wife, his bosses, his roadmender's cart? To forget them all and make a new and better life elsewhere? And why had he come back? Remorse? Poverty? Force of habit? It was lucky for him that M. Arnaldon, the Mayor, had managed to get him reinstated by pleading his status as the head of a large family.

Joigneau passed the last houses of the village, and came, almost at once, to the cemetery. In the middle of the tombs stood the war memorial: a granite soldier who smiled as he charged with the bayonet. He and Joigneau were old friends: he served, in fact, as a sort of barometer. On wet days he turned black; if it was misty he turned the colour of slate; but if the sun shone out he was all blue – sky-blue, as was only right: and his helmet glittered.

Joigneau pedalled harder, to get across the little wooden bridge over the Yeulette; next came the ride across the island, that ever-moist little strip of marshland that lay squeezed between the larger and the smaller arms of the river. It was still bathed in the vapours of first light. Then Joigneau had to pedal hard once again to get over the Yeule. The steep-backed bridge was of stone. And last came the climb up to the station, between the crow-haunted fields. The countryside had its early morning look: cleanly, it seemed, and patient. Tumultuous birdsong announced that the day would be one of great heat; but the heat was still high in the sky, and on the road the air was soft and still, and almost cool, like a fine day in spring. On the banks the dusty grass, cropped close by sheep and scorched by the sunshine of the previous day, seemed to have recovered its green during the night-long truce; the dew, too, had played its part.

Joigneau strode up the hill, with his head low and the bicycle by his side. He knew every step of the road – every rut, every patch of repair, every heap of stones, every bush. Nothing came between him and his thoughts. But where the road turned he always stopped for a few moments and cast a proprietary glance at the slopes of the Bois-Laurent – at the exact spot, in fact, where his own vineyard was to be found, between a big heavy-leaved walnut tree and a row of free-standing peach trees.

The train got in at five to the hour. The postman was always there in good time. In twelve years he and the train had only missed each other once – by three minutes: on the day when Joigneau had thought that the bakery was on fire. Just *what* the Merlavignes and their little maid had put into their furnace on that particular night had never been discovered. It certainly hadn't been ordinary firewood; or stale crusts, either. A litter of kittens, some people

thought? It might have been; it smelt like scorching
carrion.

And then came the station, on the side of the hill. A
wisp of smoke rose up from the roof among the leafy
branches of the plane trees. The stationmaster, a
bachelor, was lighting a fire for his coffee.

2

The waiting-room had been closed all night and smelt of pipe smoke and dirty linen.

At the goods end of the station Flamart, the herculean ganger, was loading his trolley with baskets of early vegetables. Loutre, the market-gardener, produced these every morning, with the help of his assistant, from the back of a little lorry.

Joigneau walked over to the three men.

'Going to be hot on that road soon, if I know anything about it!'

'Bloody awful weather!' said the sweating Hercules, not stopping his work.

Loutre took care not to agree, though the sweat was pouring down his face. The hotter the sunshine, the better things are for a market-gardener; he only has to keep on watering. Loutre had a well in the middle of his holding that had never been known to dry up.

Flamart dragged the sweet-smelling melons towards the weighing-machine. Loutre made off to the stationmaster's office to fill in his forms.

The postman, left alone with Loutre's assistant, rolled a cigarette, and took his time about it.

'Yes, it's going to be hot on that road, Fritzy. You mark my words.'

The other man finished fastening down the tarpaulin.

'Hot, yiss. . . .'

Fritzy was a Bavarian who'd stayed on at the end of the war. He was an odd-looking fellow who looked as if he'd grown up lopsided, with a head that was too big for him and was always lolling over on to his shoulder. The long white neck reminded you of one of those weakly hens that become the martyrs of the farmyard. But the eyes were the eyes of a dreamer, and the face itself, framed by the beard of a renaissance Christ, was pleasant enough. When he sat down on the platform and sang quietly to himself, his straw hat became him like a halo. His bronzed features bore a look of complete indifference as he turned to the postman; and he went on smiling as he repeated, like a man in a dream:

'Hot, yiss, very hot, Môzieu Jagneau. . . .'

*   *   *

The postman went over to Flamart. The ganger was alone, in front of his weighing-machine, manipulating the weights. He counted aloud, so as not to make a mistake. 'Two hundred and fifty-two plus twenty – two hundred and seventy-two . . .' The flesh on his ram-like face looked as if it had been boiled. His eyes were sunk deep between the great pad of his forehead and the forward thrust of the cheekbones. They were round, small, blue, and stupid – with the stupidity of the drunkard and the man of one idea.

'I'd like a word with you,' he said, when he'd finished his weighing.

Joigneau followed him towards the lamp-room.

A station, in general, is open to all. The ganger had managed to keep, for his private use, this one reeking corner, with its filthy rags and sooted lamps, in which he could drink at his ease and abandon himself to his obsession. Every morning, before the first train arrived, he took the postman there for a little snack. His wife looked after him very well; there was always enough for two. Joigneau made the most of it; for the last year he'd made a big saving on his own sandwiches.

Flamart spread the soot-blackened table with bread, a litre of wine, and a tin of sardines that he opened with one twist of a screw-driver. The two men sat down to their meal. Outside, above the transom, a bell gave a half-hearted tinkle.

'Just left Mézu,' said Joigneau.

Each held his long slice of bread in the hollow of his left hand. They set about their food with the ancient and stately gestures of ritual. Turn and turn about, Flamart first and then Joigneau speared a sliver of oily flesh with the point of his knife, spread it on his bread, cut off a large cube and thrust it neatly into his mouth: and then, before beginning the laborious task of mastication, each in turn took care to wipe his moustache with the back of his hand.

The ganger stopped eating and bent towards the postman:

'Heard the latest? She's got an idea she wants to clean out the attic.'

Joigneau thought for a moment, with his knife in the air:

'What for?'

'To make a room. She thinks she could let it.'

Flamart raised his strangler's hands in front of his great chest and clasped them together till the joints cracked:

'But I say No!'

Joigneau, a man of caution, kept the conversation general:

'You'd have to get a licence?'

'That's not the point. She's gone into it all, the bitch. Knows more about it than you and me. With all expenses paid, she says, I'd make at least three hundred or three hundred and fifty francs a month. Think of that!' He gave Joigneau time to appreciate the extent of his sacrifice, and then repeated, his jaw set: 'But I say No!'

'Well . .' said the postman.

For a moment or two they stared one another in the face till you'd have thought they hated each other, whereas really they were each trying to find out what the other was thinking. But cleverer men than Flamart had despaired of reading Joigneau's thoughts. His faun's mask never gave him away; the eyes were doubly protected – by the shadow of his brow and the arched crevice of his eyelids; and as for the expression of his mouth, it was tucked away for good and all behind his gendarme's moustache. Very slowly, like some complicated machine that has to ease all its cogs into action, he got down to chewing again. But Flamart couldn't; so deep was his disquiet that he no longer cared even to eat.

Flamart had been in the infantry, as an N.C.O. He married a girl in a garrison town, and she found him his job on the railway. She herself ran a shop about two and a half miles from the station; it was a little shack that stood by itself at a point where three roads met. Motorists pulled up there. The shutters were always half-closed. Inside, people said, there was no limit to what went on. The bitch, as Flamart sometimes called her, could cuckold her man the whole day long. Flamart knew that very well. But though he was eaten away with suspicion, the time-table held him captive and there was nothing he could do but suffocate with rage in the lamp-room. And, besides, the bitch knew her business; the shop took a lot of money; so much, in fact, that Flamart had never thought seriously of giving it up. It was during the previous year that he had taken the postman into his confidence, in the hope that her letters, at least, would then be under surveillance. It cost him half his early morning meal. In exchange, Joigneau, the most prudent of accomplices, occasionally allowed him to read a harmless postcard.

'The ones who come and go just can't be helped,'

Flamart said suddenly. 'But if I let one of them set up house with us, I'm just done for.'

His neck went purple. His eyes rolled. Visions tormented him. An unexpected gobbling noise came up from his chest:

'He'd get her away from me!'

Joigneau gave a scornful laugh. He was wrong to do it: sharp-eyed as he was, and quick on the scent, he had not realised that when the big man's lips trembled it was from distress, rather than from rage, and that the strange gobbling sound was a cry of pain.

Above the transom, the bell fell suddenly silent. The train was coming.

Flamart got up, wiped his pocket-knife on the bread, and folded it up.

'I thought I'd tell you about it, you see, before you started your rounds, so you could put in a word from yourself when you see her.'

'Yes, I could,' said Joigneau.

He smiled to himself. He'd meant to drop by at the shop, anyway; he'd something to say to Madame Flamart.

*   *   *

A glass door opened, and the stationmaster, with his brass-buttoned uniform, stepped out on to the platform.

'Morning, chief!' said the postman.

The old man raised two fingers to the peak of his cap, from habit.

'Good morning, Joigneau.'

He was cordial, but not familiar. He carried his responsibilities sadly. Round-shouldered, his hands behind his back, his profile like that of a wind-cutter, he went off, as always, to meet his train.

*　　*　　*

From the compartment labelled POSTES a man in shirt-sleeves leant out. He was holding a padlocked bag.

Joigneau gave him one in exchange:

'Morning, Bergeon! You've got the coolest job today!'

The other was an old man, and frail in appearance. He leaned on the window-frame, knocked out his pipe into his hand, spat, and didn't answer.

Farther along the train, the baskets had been put aboard. Flamart was running with sweat. The engine whistled. The train was moving off when someone cried out. Flamart had just time to dive into the guard's van and whip out a crate of dishevelled half-dead hens. As they fell on the ground they gave a last despairing cluck.

Joigneau got on to his bicycle.

The stationmaster went back to his papers, and Flamart to his lamp-room.

On the deserted platform, in the sunshine, the hens, now at their last gasp, huddled together in their crate and went on with the business of dying.

3

The town hall clock had barely struck half-past six before the village began to rouse itself. Age-old custom, more powerful even than idleness, pulled the people from their beds and set them running to and fro like squirrels in a cage.

In the kitchen behind the post office, La Mélie, now soap-fresh, was bustling about; and nibbling, as she did so, a hunk of bread that she had rubbed in some lard. What was it that made her so appetising? Her healthy teeth, her curls, her thin white bodice, or her tripping walk? Though plump and short-legged, she was amazingly light on her feet.

Joigneau was working in his garden. He didn't begin his deliveries till nine o'clock.

La Mélie took advantage of this respite in order to clamber up to the loft and make the apprentice's bed. This wasn't included in the rent; but, after all, he was only sixteen. And if somebody didn't look after him. . . . Every morning, without exception, La Mélie went up and shook out the sheets in which Joseph had slept, and turned over the feather mattress which still bore the warm print of his body.

*　　　*　　　*

No bachelor – unless he takes a vicious delight in slavery – can combine the functions of postman and postmaster. He must have a wife. And his wife must look after the office. Joigneau had trained La Mélie. The hardest part had been to persuade her that they could never have children; a woman thinks her pregnancies important, just like any other female animal. Yet anyone can see that motherhood is incompatible with an orderly postal service. La Mélie had wept many a night through, until finally Joigneau said that she could breed puppies instead. (Besides, he could sell them; it all brought in money.)

In other respects, La Mélie had soon got into the swim. She knew how to receive and despatch a telegram, how to consult the tariffs, and how to keep her many books in order.

Despite its iron bars and dirty windows, the post office was not a prison. The lower part of the walls had been treated with saltpetre; but the upper part was covered with official notices and enlivening posters. The smell was quite pleasant; it was like that of all public buildings. And people were always coming in and out; you couldn't be bored for long.

*　　　*　　　*

The church was not, of course, in step with the town hall. The municipal clock made it ten minutes past seven before Mademoiselle Verne decided to ring the church bells.

Mademoiselle Verne, the Curé's sister, kept the

keys of the church; she hid them at night beneath her bolster. Each morning it was she who opened the little door in the transept and was the first to walk beneath the echoing vault. It was a moment of incomparable pride. God belonged to her, and her alone: and He spoke to her, as to His favourite. She alone was privileged to break the holy silence of the nave with the clatter of her clogs on the stone floor; and it was she, too, who hung from the bell-ropes and forced the still-slumbering village to take note of the Angelus. Her brother did not join her till she had rung for Mass. As he opened the sacristy and prepared the altar, two shadows, one after another, came slipping between the pillars and knelt behind Mademoiselle Verne: these were Mademoiselle Massot and La Celestine.

These three holy women came every morning to Mass. And, as the Curé had no one to serve him on week-days, they had the pleasure of giving the responses, turn and turn about, each taking her own day.

If God were to call any one of them to His bosom, the survivors would share her turn of duty; but this was so reprehensible a notion that they rejected it whenever it came into their heads.

When the bell went for Mass, Joigneau put away his tools and went into his office.

He emptied his bag on the big black table and adjusted his spectacles. He enjoyed sorting. All Maupeyrou lay before him, with its little secrets of the moment; Joigneau never wearied of dipping into them. Taking the envelopes one by one, he examined them for as long as was necessary; then he brought his wet stamp down sharply on the back of each and placed them according to the unchanging itinerary of his round. His instinct rarely erred; in most cases he knew more or less what lay in his hand. After twelve years a man with any flair at all will have learnt to take note, and refer back, and remember, and guess.

But just occasionally he stopped dead, with a letter poised in his finger-tips. He turned it over, felt the weight of it, held it up to the light, and sniffed it. If it refused to yield up its secrets, Joigneau did not insist; he knew that he would have the last word. Instead of putting it back with the others, he slipped it quickly into his coat-pocket. He and that letter would settle their accounts later, and in private; the envelope does not exist which sooner or later, when exposed to torture by boiling water, will not decide to confess.

4

At eight o'clock sharp Joigneau made off across the square, with his mail-bag slung over his shoulder, his képi to one side of his head and his two spaniels at his heels. He crossed the school courtyard, went into the empty classroom and called out:

'Monsieur Ennberg!'

The schoolmaster came out at once for his letters – and for those, too, for the town hall. He didn't like Joigneau to go into the kitchen, where his family were having their breakfast. Never had Monsieur Ennberg offered the postman a cigarette; never had he offered the spaniels a bone. Joigneau didn't like him. Not that he had anything against him or his ideas; it was just that he was a cold fish from the East.

Joigneau gone, the schoolmaster went back to his kitchen. Cloths were drying above the stove. The narrow room smelt of boiled milk, washing-up, and drains. The noise of the three children crowded together at the end of the table was like chicks at feeding time. Madame Ennberg, in her loose jacket, laughing and scolding by turns, filled their out-stretched bowls with a small ration of tapioca. She was a brunette, and physically so gross that even her skin and her hair seemed to drip fat. Repeated child-bearing had ruined her figure; and – what was worse – it had released, one by one, like demons, all the vulgarest instincts of her nature.

Monsieur Ennberg sat down in silence, unfolded his paper, and propped it up between his sister's bowl and his own.

*　　　*　　　*

Monsieur Ennberg and his sister looked alike. Both were thin, pale, and fair. Both had the same look of limpid short-sightedness, the same jaw, set like a pike's, and the same way of talking through half-clenched teeth. The same sarcastic smile, and the same slightly scornful way of laughing with their mouths closed and little snorts coming down their nostrils.

It was a great piece of luck that the schoolmistress of Maupeyrou should have been M. Ennberg's sister. And, furthermore, that she should never have married and could therefore help with the family's expenses. And, finally, that she should have made over to her sister-in-law the greater part of her salary, the freedom of her kitchen, and the attic in which the elder of her nieces slept. But for all this the schoolmaster, his wife and his three children would have been very uncomfortable in the apartment (one room, kitchen, and lavatory) which was allotted to them by the state.

As they pored over the organ of their party, Monsieur Ennberg and his sister, united in their hopes, their fears, and their indignations, shared the news of a world whose organisation seemed to them, if anything, grotesque rather than wicked. From time to time, with no sign exchanged, they would simultaneously shrug their pointed shoulders and give vent to a nasal laugh.

'Mum!' cried the elder of the little girls.

Madame Ennberg snatched up her youngest child, opened the door that gave on to the little side-street, bent over the threshold and held the baby out at arm's length above the steps, while it kicked out freely in the sunshine.

'And I've not got a dry nappy to put on her,' she sighed, as she straightened up. 'Well, perhaps all that'll change if M. Arnaldon gets in. . . .'

Monsieur Ennberg was quite aware of the connection which existed in his wife's mind between her children's wardrobe and the election of the mayor to the county council. She hoped that her husband would be promoted to a better-paid post. Twenty times a day she reproached him for taking no steps to this end. But the schoolmaster knew that he was very unlikely to find any village to which his sister could also be appointed; and his sister's presence meant more to him than even he himself realised; their mutual understanding, their mutual affection, and their shared faith compensated him, in some degree, for the daily disappointments to which he was exposed by his marriage, his career, and the reluctance of society to evolve in the way that he wished.

*　　　*　　　*

Punctually at half-past eight Monsieur and Mademoiselle Ennberg wiped the blackboard clean in their
respective classrooms, and school began. But up till
nine o'clock there was a continual clatter of wooden
shoes as their pupils banged to and fro. Originally
every late-comer had been punished. But then their
parents had protested, in a body, and the mayor had
at once upheld their protests – although he invariably
proclaimed on prize days, to the approval of these
very same families, that the Republic had inalienable
duties towards the children of its citizens and the
education which was theirs by birthright. The Enn-
bergs had to give in. As a matter of principle, they
went on giving bad marks, though these no longer
involved any penalty. To no one but them did it seem
of any importance that classes were being cut short by
half an hour; for no one but them, in the commune of
Maupeyrou, had the concept of compulsory non-
religious education any serious interest.

5

The square had three main centres of attraction: the post office, the town hall, and, most engaging of all, the CAFÉ-TABAC.

Joigneau always had something for Bosse, the proprietor of the café – even if it was only the socialist newspapers, which he got for nothing.

Joigneau pushed open the doors, and his two spaniels went in ahead of him.

'Come here, Pic! Here, Mirabole!'

The dogs were already half-buried in the refuse bin.

'Let them be,' said Madame Bosse easily.

Joigneau didn't insist. He'd long realised that a postman who breeds thoroughbred dogs can make a good thing out of his round, provided he's respected, held slightly in awe, and generally supposed to be a little absent-minded. His two spaniels knew the habits of every housewife and the exact location of every dustbin for five miles around. The delivery run served both to feed and to exercise them, and the proceeds from the sale of puppies was almost entirely net profit.

*   *   *

Even his warmest admirers on the municipal council had to admit that Bosse, the owner of the café, had a most villainous appearance: the forehead very low, the eyes those of a Batrachian, the chin formidable. He was vindictive and easily led.

He stood behind his zinc, leant over the sink, and carried on with the mysterious transference of certain liquids from one bottle to another. When Joigneau appeared he broke off this task and poured out two glasses of rum. This was his daily offering: Joigneau was a person of great influence.

Madame Bosse, who had been washing her tiled floor, plunged her cloth into the bucket and came over to the counter.

With her wings of dark hair, her piercing eyes, her sudden erratic gestures, and her blazing red nose, she looked like a black hen that was making up its mind to peck.

'Is it true, Monsieur Joigneau, what they're saying about old Madame Daigne?'

'What's that?' said Joigneau, not anxious to commit himself.

Madame Bosse went off at a tangent:

'How old is she, anyway? Must be a good seventy-six or seventy-seven?'

Joigneau was all alert, behind his wrinkled eyelids: not revealing anything, but ready to pounce on any game that presented itself.

'Look at her sores!' Madame Bosse got down to details. 'Look at the way she stinks! You can't wonder if she's worried about the future – can you, Emile?'

Bosse wasn't hurrying. He'd put in his word later. He tilted his head and poured the rum down the back of his throat.

Silence fell.

Madame Bosse realised that she'd have to show her hand:

'People say she's thinking of selling her place? And giving the Quérolles the money in exchange for board and lodging? D'you think it's true, Monsieur Joigneau?'

'I've heard it said,' Joigneau admitted.

Bosse said, in a voice edged with malice:

'If you ask me, it's the Curé's sister who put her up to it.'

'Well,' said Madame Bosse, suddenly tender, 'she'd be making a mistake, poor Madame Daigne. If she wants to die quietly and be looked after to the last, as a decent woman should be, she'd be going to the wrong place. It won't be that two-faced little creeping-Jesus of a Quérolle who'll do it for her.' And, with a forward plunge of her neck and her long sharp nose, she finished with: 'That's if you want *my* opinion.'

'Maybe,' said Joigneau, in the voice that he'd use for the word, 'Done!'

Husband and wife exchanged a rapid glance.

'Well, there it is,' said Madame Bosse with a sigh, as she went back to her work. 'You can't make people happy if they don't want to be. Aren't I right, Emile?'

Joigneau finished his rum, got his bag into position, whistled to his dogs: but he didn't move his elbow from the counter.

Bosse leant forward:

'Look here, Joigneau. You know me. I don't know what we'd get for it – Madame Daigne's villa, I mean – but I'll tell you one thing that's as sure as we're standing here. The man who makes the old girl change her mind is going to get ten per cent as soon as the contract's signed.'

'Never mind about that,' said Joigneau with infinite dignity. 'People like you and me don't need to go into that sort of thing. If I can do you a good turn I'll be glad to do it.' His sly little eyes grew even smaller in the slit of his eyelids and his voice was quite gentle as he went on. 'I know we'll always be able to settle things friendly-like.'

The two men clasped hands, as if concluding a treaty.

6

The baker's and the grocery are more or less exactly opposite each other. But the baker's must, in some way, exert a stronger magnetic pull upon those who leave the café – for Joigneau always, and instinctively, delivered at the Merlavignes' before going on to Madame Xavier.

That night it had been the younger Merlavigne's turn to make the bread; and it was the elder of the two who served in the shop – or, rather, who watched Ernestine, the shop-girl (an unkempt little slut, not yet sixteen), as she did the selling.

The elder of the twins could be distinguished by a wart on his left eyelid. In other respects they were identical: hook-nosed, pale-faced, goat-bearded, with grizzled hair that, like their jerseys, was never quite free from flour.

Business was bad. They couldn't compete with the big bakery in Villegrande, whose van, with a load of still-warm loaves, pulled up morning and evening in the square by the church. Their salesman gave good weight, allowed a certain amount of credit, and didn't eye the customers. Things were different at the Merlavignes', where they looked as glum as could be, insisted on ready money, stared lasciviously at every woman who entered the shop, and as often as not sold stale loaves that had been damped and put back in the oven. The only people who still went to them were their nearest neighbours, and they only did it from fear of reprisals. Joigneau knew it would all end badly: not long ago he'd investigated a suspicious letter that he'd found in his box: an anonymous and menacing letter, addressed to the director of the Villegrande bakery. The Merlavignes might be up to anything. The whole village was scared of them, without knowing quite why. None of the local girls would serve in their shop. The Villegrande labour exchange had to send them little trollops like Ernestine; they kept them shut up for six months, trained them in secret to submit to their whims, and then suddenly sent them back to Villegrande in exchange for fresher meat.

*   *   *

Madame Xavier, the grocer, was already seated at the far back of her shop, her gaze set and her hands in the hollow of her apron. She made no movement when Joigneau entered. It was only for her customers that she got up: and when Joigneau brought her her newspaper she considered that it was she who was the postman's customer.

Madame Xavier was slightly mad. That was quite clear. Even in repose, her face seemed to writhe and twitch beneath its untidy grey hair. She walked in her sleep; her daughter locked her in, at night, lest she go

B

out and frighten her neighbours. More than one good lady of the village, without going so far as to claim that Madame Xavier was a witch on the medieval scale, was convinced that her eyes could cast an evil spell; and never would an expectant mother set foot in her shop.

Madame Xavier's nature was rather like that of a cat. (She loathed cats, by the way, and drove them out of her shop.) Like a cat, she enjoyed sitting, motionless and vigilant, in an eternal daydream; and, also like a cat, she seemed to have an inner life which no human being could penetrate. When she passed through a door – even the door of her room, which she entered twenty times a day – she had an instinctive, momentary hesitation, a suspicious glance to right and to left. In shop and kitchen alike, she sat like a sentinel: back to the wall, as far as possible from the door, and so placed that she could always see who came in and out. And when she began to eat, even if it were a ragout which she had just made herself, she sniffed her plate and tasted the first mouthful in the forefront of her mouth, as if half-expecting it to be poisoned.

It was no fun to live with Madame Xavier. Hope, her lovely daughter, had dreamed of marriage long before she was ready for it, as a prisoner dreams of release. She waited in vain. She was too pretty. She had no money, and was known to read a fashion magazine every week. The boys flocked round her: but none would ever propose.

7

Although it had only two windows, Madame Daigne's little house had been called a villa from the moment the builder sketched it out on squared paper. Madame Daigne, now a woman of property, had then been sweating over a stove in the house of a lawyer in the county town. But the honorary title of 'villa' had not really been adopted in the neighbourhood until some little time later: not, in fact, till there had been added to the house a glass-roofed porch, in the 'marquise' style, above the front door. This door was itself yellow in colour, in imitation of light oak, and ornamented with silver-plated fittings like a rich man's coffin. The title was confirmed when Joigneau, with his usual geniality, displayed throughout the village an envelope which some facetious person, in writing to the ex-cook, had addressed to: Madame Daigne, Villa Rake-Off.

*   *   *

Madame Daigne lay on her bed, in skirt and camisole. For the last ten years she had been afflicted with a fistula. There was no hiding her affliction. The visitor could not but notice it from the moment he crossed the threshold of the villa. Her room was dirty, but ambitiously furnished: a wardrobe with a looking-glass, and a square piece of moquette in front of an armchair adorned with a crochet-work antimacassar.

'Sorry to bother you, Madame Daigne – and for so little, too, I'm afraid. Just a prospectus. . . . But that's what I'm here for, you know.'

(Joigneau always carried a prospectus or two for use when he wished, for one reason or another, to gain access to somebody's house.)

'Ah, Monsieur Joigneau, I'm in a bad way. Just listen and see if I'm not. My varicose veins are so bad that I can't even do my own cooking. I'd bought such a nice little sheep's head: with a vinaigrette sauce and a little tarragon it's so refreshing in this hot weather. . . . But the worms got to it before I did. D'you know that yesterday, for my supper, it was all I could do to dip a couple of biscuits in a glass of wine? I hadn't the strength to stand up. Well, that's how the world is. Money won't help you, and a nice house won't help you, Monsieur Joigneau, if you lose the use of your legs.'

'No one could say you've not got a nice house, Madame Daigne,' said Joigneau, sitting down as far as possible from the bed. 'They'd be liars if they did. But all the same, at your age, and with your illness, I'd rather see you somewhere in the centre of things, with people around you who could help you out, and not alone in this lovely villa like you are now.'

The old woman shot a glance of suspicion at the

postman. Her withered flesh formed pockets beneath
her eyelids; there was a wisp of grey beard on her
chin; and under her white cotton open-work bonnet,
there were places where the scanty hair revealed the
skull itself, as pink as the flesh of a piglet.

'Why d'you say that, Monsieur Joigneau? You're
thinking of the Quérolles?'

'The Quérolles?'

Joigneau looked so frank and open that she was
almost sorry she'd spoken. But, after all, Joigneau
was a man of experience, a man who could give good
advice.

'Ah, Monsieur Joigneau, I love my house. You
wouldn't believe how much it means to me. That's
what makes it so dreadful. . . . I could never live with
other people.'

'Is that what you were thinking of, Madame
Daigne? The Quérolles? It just shows you what
gossip is. I'd heard it was the Bosses.'

The old woman's eyes opened wider:

'The Bosses?'

'Yes. And, to tell you the truth, I didn't like the
sound of it. But the Quérolles! That's something quite
different. It'd be in their little summer-house, would
it? You couldn't do better. Of course it'd be a little
damp at the end of the garden, but varicose veins
aren't like rheumatism, you know. Damp doesn't
affect them, from what I've heard. And all you'd need
to do would be to keep a good fire going all the year
round.'

'With the Bosses?' the old woman repeated. Her eyebrows had gone up so high that you'd have thought they'd never come down.

'You don't want to bother with the Bosses, Madame Daigne, if you've got the Quérolles' summer-house. You could go for miles around and not find anything better for peace and quiet. Why, you could be there for days on end, for weeks I might say, without seeing so much as a donkey pass by, let alone a Christian. And then at your age you've got to be careful what you eat. The Quérolles are thrifty, steady-going people. They don't go in for heavy meals. Soup and a bit of cheese are enough for them. You don't need to be afraid of them ruining your stomach with a lot of showy sauces and such.'

'And what about the Bosses?'

'Now don't you go on thinking about the Bosses, Madame Daigne! They'd be just the opposite of what you need. To begin with you don't want to live right on the main square. It's too noisy for someone of your age. You'd be looking through your curtains all the time to see what was going on. And then, a café – why it's nothing but people coming and going, nothing but commotions and singing and the mechanical piano and I don't know what besides! You don't want all that noisy stuff when you get old. And I haven't come to the worst yet: the food, I mean.'

'What's wrong with that, Monsieur Joigneau?'

'You know what good food is, Madame Daigne. People always say there's no one knows more about it than you do. It's not easy to say "no" when there's something tasty on the table and people press you to take more and more, as if every day was a wedding day. Where good food's concerned the Bosses stop at nothing, believe me. If you could see what Madame Bosse throws out for my dogs – why, they get meat that you and I would be glad to keep for our Sunday dinners!'

Joigneau got up.

'You mark my words, Madame Daigne: don't start thinking of the Bosses. I'd blame myself for the rest of my life if I thought I'd put that idea into your head. And now I must be off. I hope you'll be better soon, Madame Daigne, and I'd like to think of you, safe in the hands of decent people like the Quérolles.'

'Just a moment, Monsieur Joigneau. Could you kindly bring me that blue bottle from the side-table? You're not in such a hurry as all that – drink a glass with me, do.'

'If it's to give you pleasure, I won't say no, Madame Daigne. Besides, you'd better make the most of it while you can. There'll be none of that at the Quérolles'. You'll be out of reach of these evil temptations. They're teetotallers, you know; they subscribe to the League, like the Curé. . . .'

'The League?'

'Why yes, as sure as I'm sitting here. She's a woman of principle, Madame Quérolle. She sends her little contribution every year to the League of Total Abstainers.'

The old woman made a great effort and sat upright on the edge of her mattress. She could only stammer the words:

'Goodness gracious me! The League of Total Abstainers?'

8

Monsieur Ferdinand, *coiffeur-parfumeur*, was watching his son Francis spread fresh sawdust round the one armchair which graced his shop.

'Morning, Ferdinand!' said the postman. 'Here are your filthy rags!'

Monsieur Ferdinand was an active member of an extreme right-wing .party, and his customers were offered only the stuffiest and most respectable of papers.

He was a little pot-bellied fellow, whose grey moustache was freshly ironed each morning. He was bald; but hid his baldness beneath a wig, for fear that it might affect the sale of his hair lotions.

He was the son, the grandson, and the great-grandson of barbers; and it was a great grief to him that he should have sired a rebel, an emancipated little squirt whose hair was as stiff as chalk and who cared nothing at all for the traditions of his family.

'There's no *feeling* in your scissors,' Monsieur Ferdinand would say, in despair. For it was his belief that you could tell a born hairdresser by the click of his scissors, which should be as cheerful as a carillon on Easter Day. He himself bore this out: his scissors chirped and capered at his fingers' ends, till their perpetual spring-song nearly deafened his clients.

He loved his art, and he knew it through and through. Cut-throat and safety-razor came equally easily to him; but the latter method, though more modern, was not much in demand in Maupeyrou, where it was regarded as costly and ineffective. Moreover, in using the cut-throat, Monsieur Ferdinand so far respected the demands of hygiene as to pass his thumb beneath the cold tap before placing it under his customer's cheek.

The café-tabac was the acknowledged centre of the anti-clerical left; and as there was no other café in Maupeyrou the conservatives had chosen to set up their headquarters in Monsieur Ferdinand's shop – although, in point of fact, and as everybody had to be shaved on Saturday and liked to go somewhere for a drink on Sunday, the partisans of one side and the other were constantly meeting, either in the café or at the barber's.

The left had also another reason to keep in with Monsieur Ferdinand: Madame Ferdinand was the local midwife – the only one in the region. A woman renowned for the strength of her biceps, she exercised her profession without regard for political distinctions, and cut the umbilical cords of the left as dexterously as those of the right.

*   *   *

Except on market days, the ironmonger's was empty. Joigneau took care never to see the all-too-holy Quérolles. A bell rang automatically as he crossed the threshold of the shop; but before anyone could come out from the back the letters were on the table and the postman safely away.

Lazy hogs, Madame Bosse called them. They did less than any other family in Maupeyrou, and would never be forgiven for it. Quérolle didn't mind putting in a few minutes in the shop, or in the kitchen garden, when it was cool; but in the heat of the day he took his siesta. His wife sat from morning till night in the kitchen, hemming her napkins, mending dishcloths, and cutting up worn-out sheets to make underclothes for her daughter Lucie. Lucie was a great gawky bespectacled creature who detested needlework and was always hiding in corners, the better to read the books which she was lent by the schoolmistress.

The Quérolles – the husband and wife, that is to say – had been brooding for three months on the best way of capturing old Madame Daigne. Linen was Madame Quérolle's passion, and her supreme object was to lay hands on the old woman's linen-cupboard. As for her husband, he had worked it out a hundred times that, 'What with the sale of the villa . . . and the old woman's board and lodging . . . why, even at the worst, even if she lived for another five or six years, we'd still make a clear profit of . . .'

*   *   *

Although Joigneau rarely visited Mademoiselle Célestine, the two spaniels made a point of sneaking quickly inside and drinking the milk which she put out for her cat.

But that morning the door was shut. Célestine must have finished her housework early.

No . . . Célestine hadn't got up.

She was sitting in her bed. Weeping.

A tragedy had happened.

On midsummer's day she had gone to the fairground and had there lost the necklace of medals that she had worn since her first communion. How could she ever find it, in such a crowd – she who never went out? And just then the Devil had whispered in her ear. Without a word to anyone, she had lit a blessed candle, and made a vow: 'O good St Anthony, give me back my medals, and I will put up a statue of you in our church.' The next day a little shepherd's boy brought her back her medals. She ordered from Villegrande a statue to the value of forty francs, and promised to pay at the end of the month. And then, the night before, she had heard the news. Madame Quérolle, the ironmonger's wife, had arranged with the Curé that *she* would erect a statue to St Anthony in the village church! The statue had been carried right through the village on a cart: and in a case that you could see through. The Quérolles had put it in the shed in their courtyard. It was a life-size St Anthony, people said, and painted in colours.

Célestine had spent the night on her knees, in a holy

trance. Nobody was to blame. She'd not taken anyone into her confidence: had wished, in fact, to give Monsieur le Curé a surprise. But you couldn't have two St Anthonys in the same church. . . .

She wept, and felt herself damned.

* * *

Suddenly she raised her head, jumped out of bed, and climbed up into her attic without even waiting to put on a skirt. She pulled herself up to the skylight, and peered over across the rooftops and down into a narrow alleyway. There was a low hedge; and, a little further away, a shed; and, between the hedge and the shed, a heap of dry logs. With a match, and a screw of paper . . .

For a moment or two she stood there, petrified, with craning neck. The flames were already darting from her eyes. . . .

The shed was the Quérolles'.

9

The presbytery had a yard in front of it, and a garden behind. Anyone who rang the door-bell was faced with Mademoiselle Verne. For this reason the bell was hardly ever rung.

Mademoiselle Verne was a curé's sister, elderly, indiscreet, exemplary, and a virgin. She kept the parish in order; she loathed most of the villagers, and was as heartily loathed by them; and against her enemies she launched, with many an imperious word of command, the little resistance group of pure reactionaries which every church harbours somewhere within its shadow.

* * *

Even in winter-time Joigneau was sure to find the priest in his garden if he went down the little lane and looked for him. He stood upright on his pedals and called across the hedge:

'Monsieur Verne!'

The priest shuddered from head to foot, dug his spade in the ground, and came over with the convulsive waddle which, in recent years, distinguished his gait even when he climbed up to his pulpit. ('It's not a priest we've got,' said Pascalon, the grave-digger. 'It's a Punch and Judy show.')

The Abbé Verne raised his straw hat in courteous salute and took his letters. These letters were usually a day late. Joigneau honoured the Curé's correspondence with a particular surveillance. The Abbé Verne guessed as much; and accepted and forgave it, as much from indifference as from charity.

*   *   *

The Abbé Verne was an old man, dark-skinned, with warmth in his eye; but skinny, and afflicted with a nervous illness.

Thirty-five years earlier he had arrived in Maupeyrou with the luggage of a seminarist and the zeal of a young apostle. He was faced with an ancient countryside which was set in its ways. His parishioners thought only of themselves, and of their little businesses, their little savings, and their hopes of security. At the beginning he had done his utmost to break down their indifference to religion and to foster among his charges a spirit of practical Christianity. It had been a waste of time. Even the church-goers evaded his advances. The village club, the charity school, the committee for good works – all were founded on paper: all came to nothing, for lack of recruits. For too many generations his parishioners had been parsimonious in all things: whatever instincts of generosity they might once have had were now atrophied. They were a suspicious, envious, calculating race; cupidity stalked among them like a cancer. Had it always been so? It was a question which the priest often put to himself in anguish. For centuries, after all, the common people of France had come to kneel in the church which now they were deserting. What had brought them there? Faith? Some spiritual need which now no longer existed? . . . Or was it rather from fear? Fear of God, and of the clergy? The habit of respect for an established order? The Abbé Verne knew he could no longer count on such levers – even if their use had not been repugnant to him.

Little by little this general indifference had got the better of his courage, his patience, and his health. And so he turned in upon himself, and lived according to Trappist rules of his own devising. His refuge was the kitchen-garden. A solicitous Providence had made it large, well-watered, and fertile. He worked in it for ten hours a day. And as his stipend was absurdly small he grew early vegetables and sold them (for very little) to Loutre; in this way he kept alive, and could even distribute a little alms from time to time.

The presbytery, the church, and in the end the parish itself he had yielded over, without a struggle, to the vociferous despotism of his sister. He was never seen in church except at the hours appointed for Mass. Every Sunday, at High Mass, no matter how small the attendance, his conscience drove him to climb up into his pulpit and to speak, as best he could, to the women and old maids who remained faithful to Mademoiselle Verne and to God.

* * *

One of the presbytery windows was opened with a bang.

'Come at once!' called Mademoiselle Verne.

The Curé straightened up from his gooseberry bushes, put down his basket, and made haste to button his soutane.

He found Mademoiselle Célestine slumped on a chair, near the stove, in a flood of tears.

'Monsieur le Curé, I made my vow first, I really did!'

Mademoiselle Verne, ever ready to sound her neighbours' hearts and judge the state of their consciences, gave a running commentary on the situation with her usual voluble self-confidence.

'Now don't get upset,' said the Curé to Célestine. 'I have full authority to release you from your vow. You can present something else to the church – a Joan of Arc, for instance . . . and that will do just as well.'

But Célestine only wrung her hands and wept all the more. The idea of a Joan of Arc appalled her.

'St Anthony would never understand, Monsieur le Curé. He'd make me lose everything I have, just to punish me.'

The Curé kept control of himself. But his face was ravaged – even more than usual – by tics; incapable of keeping still, he wandered round and round the two distracted spinsters.

Mademoiselle Verne blamed it all on him:

'It's all your fault! Why did you ever let the Quérolles give their statue? Go and see them at once and talk them out of it!'

*   *   *

Madame Quérolle was sewing in the kitchen, with her daughter Lucie beside her. The room was full of flies and smelt of cabbage.

Madame Quérolle offered him a chair.

'Sit down, Monsieur le Curé. . . .' And she thought to herself: 'Has Madame Daigne sent him here?' Just in case, she sent Lucie off into the garden to fetch a lettuce.

The Curé sat down, got up again, and decided to stay on his feet. Hopping from one foot to the other, sniffing and shrugging like a dog that's just been in the water, he explained why he had come.

'You're a woman of heart, Madame Quérolle. I want to appeal to your charity. The poor girl thinks that she's damned; she can't sleep any more; she's making herself ill. Simple people must be judged by their intentions. . . .'

Madame Quérolle grew slowly scarlet as she looked at the floor. Her arms were folded across her breast.

'Well, of course, if we'd known, we'd never have gone to the expense. . . . But what's done is done,

Monsieur le Curé. We've got the plinth all ready. We've even got our name on the plaque, as having given it!' Her voice grew shriller. 'We've paid for it. It's only natural that we want to get something for our money, isn't it?'

'But she's willing to refund all your expenses.'

'What, all of them?'

'All of them.'

That really made Madame Quérolle think it over. 'I must ask my husband.'

Quérolle had been daydreaming in bed and was still adjusting his braces as he came downstairs. He was pear-shaped – and a sleepy pear at that; his head was small and pointed; his chin seemed to have foundered in his neck, the neck to have melted into the shoulders, and the torso to have spread down to the seat of his trousers. If you sat him on the ground, nothing in the world could have knocked him over.

Apprised of the position, he exchanged a brief glance with his wife.

'Well now, Monsieur le Curé, I'm quite ready to call the whole thing off, if the good lady sees it that way. But it won't be cheap, you know. We'd wanted to do the thing well. Our statue cost every bit of two hundred francs. I'll show you the catalogue. What with the delivery and the rest of it – why, put it in round figures and call it two hundred and twenty. Paid in cash, too. You needn't worry about the plaque. I'll fix that with a bit of plaster, *gratis pro Deo. . . .*'

The Abbé Verne was twitching with delight. There was an end of the whole silly business!

Quérolle fell silent. He wanted to do the sums in his head. The statue, complete with engraved plinth, had cost him exactly one franc; Madame Quérolle had had the imprudence to take a ticket for the Christian Youth tombola, and she'd won a prize: holy objects to the value of two hundred francs. It had been delivered for nothing; but he'd had to give the lorry driver a glass of wine. Not a bad morning's work, all in all.

The best of luck of all was something he never knew: that if he'd said 'no', his shed would have been burnt down the next night.

10

Smoke rose between the houses behind the church. It came from the house of Pouillaude, the wheelwright.

Pouillaude only tyred his wheels once every three months, when he had assembled enough orders to make it worth his while. It provided a free entertainment for his neighbours. Joigneau had neither a letter nor a newspaper for Pouillaude, but he couldn't resist the temptation to go up the narrow lane and join the other spectators. There was a tremendous commotion in the yard. Pouillaude himself, assisted by his son Nicolas and Joseph the apprentice, was puffing and blowing around the enormous flaming brazier which stood, like a funeral pyre in ancient times, in the centre of the open space.

Pouillaude was an old man, built like an athlete. With his tanned face and circlet of grizzly beard, he looked like some veteran of the high seas. He'd never been known to smile. His wife had left him after fifteen years of slavery. He'd made her life unbearable; she died of consumption. He lived with his son Nicolas, who disliked his father's trade and would have liked to turn to office work instead; but he'd never dared to say so. Pouillaude was not popular.

People said, in fact, that you couldn't make friends with him. But that didn't prevent him from being famous as a wheelwright as far as Villegrande itself.

Preparations had begun on the previous day, when Pouillaude had laid out a dozen or so circles of iron on a litter of faggots and dry straw; then he'd filled in the circles with old bits of wood, and surrounded the whole with a threefold palisade of logs, until the iron itself was invisible beneath a huge round heap of logs set side by side. In the morning it only remained to pour a gallon of petrol over it all and set a match to it.

The wood creaked; black smoke shot up in long plumes, blew round the yard for a minute and then rose with the hot air and hung for a long time above the rooftops.

When Joigneau got near, the charred logs were already beginning to collapse and the iron circles, enthroned on the heaps of red embers, to be revealed to view. This was the moment for which Pouillaude had been waiting. Now his work could begin. A maniacal tyrant, he did everything himself; the two boys merely brought him things and accepted his rebuffs.

'Jump to it!' he shouted.

Nicolas and Joseph ran to fetch the first of the wheels which were to be tyred. They rolled them over to the side of the fire, laid them out on a huge star of iron, and pinned them down with a stake through the hub. Then the three men, each armed with a long piece of pointed steel, stood equidistant round the fire.

'One and two and THREE!' the old man roared.

As one man, they snatched one of the red-hot hoops from the heart of the furnace, poised it above the wheel, which was almost exactly the same size, and laid it neatly on the circumference of the wheel. As soon as it felt the red-hot iron, the wood of the wheel caught fire.

'Quick!' Pouillaude shouted.

Two barrels of water were ready within reach. Nicolas and Joseph dipped their watering-cans in these and made haste to souse the blazing wheel. There was a blinding, whistling flash of steam that drove the crowd back. The fire, drowned on one side, blazed up again on the other; the cans were filled and emptied, water gushed out everywhere, and the two boys slithered in the mud as they beat out the flames that flared up again and again all round the wheel, as soon as they were left for dead. Meanwhile Pouillaude, with the help of a long mallet, set about the iron hoop till it fitted exactly over the frame of the wheel. Quite soon the last flame had flickered out in the white circle of ash and water, and the iron hoop, contracting as it cooled, was indissolubly wedded to the wood. The first wheel had been shod.

'Hop!' the old man shouted.

The two boys carefully lifted the wheel clear of the mess; and Pouillaude slipped an iron rod through the hub and rolled it over to where a kind of gallows was standing above a tank full of water. There he hung the wheel in such a way that it could turn freely and complete the cooling process. And, sure enough, the creaking grew less and less till, in the end, the wheel spun silently round and round in the water.

Little Joseph was already played out. Exhaustion gave a look of fever to his eyes. His blue linen trousers were wet to the knees, and his shirt was stuck to his back with sweat.

'Next one!' cried the wheelwright.

'Come on, boys!' said Joigneau to his spaniels.

11

Madame Massot's home was like her way of life: austere. Nothing could be seen from the street but a high and sturdy wall, the *mur Massot*, in which was a tiny prison-door. Madame Massot and her daughter had money; but they seemed to be the only people who didn't know it. They lived, in fact, like holy paupers, and were obsessed with the fear of not being able to pay their bills.

Nothing daunted, Joigneau and his dogs forced an entrance into this clerical fortress.

In the middle of the paved courtyard that was bounded on three sides by the house, a virago of thirty-five was at work in the sun. On her head was a newspaper, folded in the shape of a cocked hat; she was cleaning a bird-cage.

'There's a registered packet for your mother, Mademoiselle. I shall have to have her signature.'

Mademoiselle Massot put down her watering-can. Astonishment and ill-will were combined in her features as she stared Joigneau in the face. Would she withdraw without a word? Or advance and put him out in the street? Either seemed possible. But in the end she shrugged her shoulders, turned on her heel,

and went up into the house. Joigneau followed her.
They passed through a flagged hall, cool as a cellar,
and began to climb an old stone staircase, whose steps
had been worn away by long use.

Madame Massot was sitting knitting. Her shutters
were closed, and she herself was shut not only in her
room, but in the inner room of her deafness. She was
dressed in a full-skirted silk dress, like somebody in a
portrait. This dress was worn out. All day long, and
indeed all night long, for she now slept hardly at all,
she counted her stitches; criss-cross and click-clack
went her long needles. For twenty-five years every
child in the village (and, during the war, every soldier
for miles around) had sweated ungratefully in socks,
pants, jerseys and scarves made by Madame Massot
with her own holy hands. On these alone did she
spend her money; thus did she buy the right to speak
of 'my poor boys'.

The old woman in her deafness did not even hear
the door open. Her daughter made her jump as she
screamed in her ear:

'It's the postman, Mother. He wants you to sign.'

The old face, paper-pale and paper-fragile, turned
in alarm towards Joigneau and then towards her
daughter.

Mademoiselle Massot understood.

'I hope there's nothing to pay?' she asked.

'No, Mademoiselle.'

'Nothing to pay,' shouted Mademoiselle Massot in
her most reassuring voice.

Madame Massot rose with surprising alacrity, pulled a bunch of keys from her pocket, tripped across the room to her desk, and opened it. Taking from it a tiny bottle of ink, she opened it with great care and probed inside it with her rusty pen.

'There . . .' said Joigneau, pointing to the blank space in his book.

The ink was so pale that he blew on her signature, not daring to blot it.

The two women exchanged another glance. No: there was no question of giving the anti-clerical postman a tip.

The canaries piped in the unshaded little court-yard, where the two spaniels, having sniffed at the cage, tasted the water in the can, and ferreted in vain for more solid nourishment, were now lying, heavy-tongued, on the hot cobbles.

Mademoiselle Massot stood at the porch to make sure that Joigneau closed and latched the street-door.

*   *   *

Nothing was known of Madame Massot when she came, with her little daughter, to live in the long-deserted house that had belonged to her husband's grandmother. Disagreeable rumours had of course been started in respect of her. But could it really be maintained that this pious old person, who was hardly ever out of the church, had sung, during the course of an adventurous youth, in the disreputable bars of Marseilles? Or that her ever-readiness in the alcove

had been the cause of the duel in which Captain
Massot had been killed, in a garrison town in
southern Algeria?

All that had happened twenty-five years previously,
and was now thoroughly forgotten. For twenty-five
years Madame Massot had lived alone with her
daughter in the old house which smelt, as did she
herself, of camphor and pigskin and the inside of
trunks that had not been opened for two generations.
The two women lived in only two of its rooms. Flies,
mice, weevils and dust had taken possession of the
tiled corridors, the hanging-cupboards with their
heaps of empty cardboard boxes, and the white rooms
with their countrified woodwork, their broken-down
chairs, their four-poster beds. Beneath the windows
were little black heaps that stirred, at the least breath
of wind, with a noise like dead leaves: these were
flies that had died of boredom.

*   *   *

Madame Massot stood in the middle of her room and
turned the registered packet over and over in her
marionette's fingers. She was waiting for the return
of her bodyguard. Whenever initiative was called for,
she put herself in the hands of her big, bony, full-
blooded daughter, who knew how to pump water,
how to saw up wood, how to polish floors, how to say
the responses at Mass, how to argue with the tax-
collector, and even, when it was needed, how to bleed a
rabbit by whipping out its eye with the point of a knife.

Mademoiselle Massot lost no time in opening the packet. But it took the two women a good quarter of an hour to realise what had happened: that the tube of lead which had come so unexpectedly into their lives was nothing but a harmless sample of toothpaste wrapped up in a chemist's prospectus.

Life, for an instant, was knocked sideways; but in the end it returned to its normal course. The mother took up her knitting; the daughter went back to her canaries.

She had about thirty canaries at that time. In spring-time she felt drawn towards their cage by some confused and disquieting emotion. Normally the most active of women, she mooned about for hours, quite motionless, and watched the nests on which the female canaries were hatching their young. When the tiny birds were out of the egg, her secret delight was to take one of them and hide it in the warmth of her bosom. She would go off to finish her work with the bird inside her and nothing to show it. Once she had even taken one to church with her!

Every day, at three o'clock in winter and five in the summer, she could be seen entering the holy place by the little door in the transept. She went straight to the confessional, and there took her tucker and apron from behind the curtain. Mademoiselle Verne was usually there before her. Taking their time, like two workwomen who loved their work and wanted to make the pleasure last, they swept the stone floor, dusted the benches, arranged the chairs neatly and

put fresh oil in the ever-burning lamp. The vigils of
the church were like bank holidays to them; for on
those days the work went on all afternoon. They had
to polish the candelabra, change the altar-cloths,
check all the ornaments, and fill every vase with
leaves and flowers. They always managed to work
side by side; and, like two washerwomen, they kept
up an uninterrupted conversation; the news of the
day was passed, item by item, through the sieve of
their high-minded austerity; but so quietly did they
talk, and so monotonously, that they might have been
reciting a litany; and even when they were speaking ill
of their neighbours they always made some semblance
of a genuflexion while passing before the Tabernacle;
a gesture of politeness that was at once respectful and
familiar, for they felt themselves part of the family.

*　　*　　*

Mademoiselle Massot was plain, but didn't know it.
She had thick wrists and ankles, the neck and shoulders
of a brood-mare, heavy eyelids, and hands that always
looked as if they were swollen with chilblains; and,
ugliest of all, a patch of black fur at either end of her
mouth. During the last few years she had often
blushed fiery red; red patches would come and go on
her neck and shoulders and arms, and perhaps, too, on
other parts of her body. She'd thought of seeing the
doctor about it, but she would die rather than undress
in front of a man. There were many reasons for this,
and the state of her underclothes was the least of them

all. When she changed these underclothes, on the first and third Sunday of each month, she always threw open the door of her glass-fronted wardrobe, lest she yield to the immodest temptation of seeing herself in the mirror; and she gripped the dirty chemise in her teeth, only letting it fall to the ground when the clean one was safely in position.

She would have been amazed if anyone had asked if she were happy. Her face bore a look of constant anxiety; sometimes a strange animation would make her eyes shine; and there was an exaggerated tenderness in the way she looked at young children.

One evening during the summer, when she had taken some baby's vests to the wife of Féju the roadmender, she returned home by the towpath along the river. Three boys had been bathing and were playing leapfrog, naked, in the grass. She had to pass between them. The eldest was no longer a child. . . .

Madèmoiselle Massot had been disturbed by this for months, and thought of it, in spite of herself, before going to sleep. It had happened quite five or six years ago; but never again had she taken that path.

12

The Loutres lived on the edge of the marshland, where it was always a little less warm than anywhere else. The market-gardener's house was pretty and well kept; it was Fritzy who repaired the roof on Sundays, repainted the shutters, and made those tiny, brightly coloured windmills that turned, in the least breath of wind, on every stake in the fence.

Joigneau pushed on the gate.

'Hullo, son!'

A boy was sitting among the heaped baskets under the lean-to, mending the hinges of the lids with oziers. He came forward into the sunlight, bent down to stroke the spaniels, and called out in a clear voice:

'Mummy!'

His high colour made his eyes seem as clear as spring water, and gave a look of whiteness to his fair curly hair.

'Do come in, Monsieur Joigneau,' said Madame Loutre from the threshold. 'The men were just saying they had something to talk to you about. Go and fetch them, Eric!'

The boy jumped over the gate and went off at a run.

The garden was divided into little squares, each

with its tiny canal that sparkled in the sun; two white-shirted figures could be seen in the distance, side by side; and as he ran to fetch them, the boy jumped, with his legs together, across the melons which lay in their cloches like so many cupping-glasses in a row.

*   *   *

Before the war of 1914, the Loutres were childless, and eked out a living by keeping a cow or two and selling the milk to the village. Then Madame Loutre had inherited the house, which was in ruins, and a small-holding of fields half-sunk in the mud.

The war had come. After a few weeks Loutre wrote home from Germany to say that he and the whole of his regiment were out of the war for good. Madame Loutre had had to fend for herself. Cattle were fetching a good price. She bought more; and she applied for a German prisoner to help her look after them.

Fritzy – for he it was – had spent the whole of his youth in a market-garden in Bavaria. He was a hard-working boy, and he saw from the start that a good thing could be made out of the semi-derelict marsh-land. The neighbours didn't believe it; but he set to work, dug ditches, drained off the water, dried out the soil, and took advantage of the lie of the land to devise a system of irrigation based on little dams of his own invention. Madame Loutre worked with him, and as hard as any man. In two years the spongy meadows had been transformed into a fertile holding, and

C

Madame Loutre, with her keen business sense, was choosing thè right markets for her produce.

The neighbours no longer laughed; the success of the venture turned their smiles to envy. And when envy gave place to hatred they revenged themselves by defaming the industrious couple. The birth of a child brought the scandal to a head; and it was with malevolent expectation that they waited for the end of the war and the return of Loutre, who was famous for his violence. What was their surprise, therefore, when the Armistice came, to find that Madame Loutre refused to banish her Fritzy!

One day Loutre arrived, without warning. Fifty-two months as a prisoner of war had turned the one-time terror of the village into a haggard, easy-going convalescent, whose one wish was to drink as much as he liked and take things easily. What did he find? His wife was plump and prosperous; his house had been rebuilt; there was plenty to eat; business was already very good; and in a wicker cradle which Fritzy had woven himself was a sturdy little boy. There was no anger in Loutre's comatose features as he took it all in. Behind his low forehead he was weighing the pros and the cons; more especially the pros.

'Don't start any nonsense,' his wife had said to him. 'If you want your cut, come in with us. Fritzy'll show you how.'

Loutre made no answer; but after a few days' rest he went quietly off to begin his apprenticeship.

It was his wife's business, after all. The banking

account was in her name. When she spoke of her husband and the Bavarian, she said 'my men', like a corporal.

There was a double bed in each of the two rooms of the house. Madame Loutre slept in one and her son in the other. As to which of her two 'men' slept with the boy, and whether it was always the same one, no one had ever discovered.

*   *   *

'You'll have something to quench your thirst, won't you, Monsieur Joigneau?' said Madame Loutre. Her peasant's features were calm and a little hard. She put a cool jug on the table and filled three glasses with a foaming liquid. 'It's Fritzy,' she said, 'who makes it for me, with rowan tree berries fermented in honey.'

The room was unlike any other room for many miles around. Joigneau never dared let his dogs inside. Furniture and floor alike were the same light waxy yellow. The daylight filtered in through fresh-painted shutters. Flowers, in little boxes of many coloured strips of wood, made the windows bright and gay. Here too, no doubt, Fritzy had made himself felt.

The two men came in – wearing slippers, because of the parquet. They were dressed alike, in clean shirts and twill trousers. But the short, stocky French peasant looked like a labourer beside the German.

'Drink it slowly. It's treacherous stuff in this heat,' said Madame Loutre in the voice of one accustomed to command. She gave a firm glance round the room and slowly withdrew.

The three men sat down at the table, in silence.

'We'd like you to do us a service, Joigneau,' said Loutre. His eyes, and his nose, that turned up at the end like the rump of a hen, made him look more cunning than he really was. 'It's about Fritzy. We'd like to have him *nationalised*.'

The Bavarian's Jesus-like head lolled over to one side as he lowered his eyes to the floor.

'Well?' said Loutre, as if Joigneau had made some gesture of surprise. 'What's against it? It'd be best for everyone.' He drank a mouthful, paused, and went on: 'We don't know how to do it, see? We'd like you to talk to the mayor and get it through for us, as quick as you can.'

Joigneau felt their eyes upon him: Fritzy's, reddish-brown, and Loutre's, blue and sharp.

'I may as well say at once, Joigneau,' Loutre went on, 'that the time you spend on it won't be time wasted. My wife agrees with me there. A service is a service. And money's money.'

'Never mind about that,' said Joigneau. 'I've a great respect for Fritzy. I'll speak to the mayor, if you like. The only thing is – it's not cheap, these days, a nationalisation.'

'Expensive, eh?'

'I should think so.'

The German once again looked down at the ground, and stroked his skinny neck with an awkward motion of his long bony fingers. Loutre too looked down for a moment as he toyed with his empty glass. Then he got up.

'In that case we'd like to know what it costs before we go any further. It's my wife who's set on it. As far as I'm concerned we needn't be in a hurry to spend the money. You go into it, and we'll see if it's worth while.'

'Right you are,' said Joigneau as he picked up his satchel.

*　　　*　　　*

Madame Loutre had been standing behind the door. Her face had grown hard, and there was a look of insistence about her as she said:

'We can count on you, can't we, Monsieur Joigneau? And here's a nice melon, a really sweet one, for your good lady's lunch.'

13

The Belgians were always awake before cockcrow; but it took them several hours to get themselves dressed. The old woman got out of bed first. She was bent at right angles and it was a long time, and an agonising one, before she could stand upright. Resting between each effort, she put on stockings and skirt.

The Belgian, her husband, watched her from his bed. He'd have liked to help her. But he needed her even more than she needed him. When, at last, she was ready, she pulled aside the sheet and dragged her man's two heavy legs clear of the mattress. Then she went behind the bed, dug her heels into the foot of the wall, put her hands beneath her husband's back and pushed with all her might: meanwhile he held on to the rope which hung from the ceiling. They encouraged one another with cries of 'Hup! Hup'! in unison. The old man's trunk rose, time and again, only to fall back. His wife grew angry and abused him, calling him heartless and selfish; sometimes she even wept from sheer discouragement. At last he got going, gave an extra-good heave, and was up on his feet. Standing up, with bare legs, knobbly knees, hook-nose, and a chin like the sole of a wooden clog, he looked like a puppet. But the worst was now over. Leaning on his stick, he made his way to the wall and propped himself up against it. His wife squatted in front of him and put on his socks and his trousers. By way of thanks, he passed his horny hand across the nape of her neck.

Clinging to one another, they tottered out into their yard – the day was beginning – the Belgians lived in their yard.

*   *   *

They had arrived in Maupeyrou in August 1914. The refugees who came with them had long since gone back. They themselves had bought the little house, some way outside the village, and had grown old there. They were polite to everyone, helped their neighbours when they could, and never quarrelled with the villagers. They were not liked. With them, people said, it was all sell and no buy. Old as she was, the wife never hesitated, even as late as the previous year, to set off on the long walk from Maupeyrou to Villegrande, if by doing so she could get a shilling more for a pair of pigeons or a basket of greengages. But now they were really old. The husband never stirred from his bed and his wicker armchair. His wife squatted near him, and got up only when it was absolutely necessary: to warm up a little soup, or to fetch a bucket of water, or to throw a handful of grain to the last survivor of the chicken-run.

*   *   *

Joigneau found them sitting in front of their
kitchen.

The yard, which had once been well kept, was now
overgrown with dust-ridden nettles. The few leaves
of an unwatered acacia dispensed a frugal shade. But
the two old people had no warmth in their veins and
did not fear the sun.

'Morning, neighbour!'

The Belgian smiled. Joigneau had called him 'neighbour' ever since he bought a little strip of vineyard, on
the slope of the Bois-Laurent, just next to that belong-
ing to the old man.

'News from home,' said Joigneau as he opened his
satchel. 'If you've no objection I'd like to have the
stamp for the stationmaster's collection.'

The old woman nodded sadly. You'd have thought
that beneath the faded black straw hat there was
nothing but a skull, rigged out with some absurd
white curls.

'It's not pleasant to grow old, Monsieur Joigneau.
Especially for people like us, seventy and more years
old, quite alone and a long way from home. . . . Sit
down a moment. We don't get many visitors here. . . .
I'm sometimes quite frightened at night, would you
believe it? And when one of us is gone – let's say it's
me, for instance – what'll become of him, with no one
to look after him? D'you know – he can't even do his
daily duty by himself?'

The old man sat quite still, his stick between
his bony old knees, and his eyes shining out at

Joigneau. Fear and shame could be read in those eyes.

'Why don't you get yourselves a servant?'

The old woman's mouth turned down at the corners.

'No, thank you! Why, we'd have to pay her wages! What little we still get, by letting off half our garden and the vines on the Bois-Laurent, would go into someone else's pocket, and a nice thing that would be! Ah, no, dear Monsieur Joigneau, we often talk about it among ourselves. What we ought to have done, while we could still get about for ourselves, was to find a girl, a good strong one, not flighty either, and say to her, "Come and live with us. We won't pay you, of course, but when we die we'll leave you everything. The house, the garden, and the bit of vineyard, and even our little savings as well!" ' She pressed her dry hands, one against the other, and sighed: 'That's what we ought to have done, Monsieur Joigneau. It's too late now. I could no more find a girl like that now than I could thread my needle without my glasses. . . .'

*   *   *

'Good God!' said Joigneau to himself. 'The house . . . the garden . . . and the vines. . . .'

He was clear of the village now, and pedalling beneath the implacable sun towards La Fourche, Madame Flamart's shop.

A young girl was sprawled on the bank, while her goat nibbled its way along the hedge. This was the

daughter of, La Mauriçotte – that being the name
given to Madame Mauriceau, the consumptive's wife.
She was well forward for her fifteen years, the
little girl; you could see that from the way her
ragged overall was stretched tight across her little
breasts.

Joigneau got down from his bicycle. He was
delighted to have an excuse for a breather.

'And how are things at home?'

She did not move as he came up. Her brown hair
was wet with sweat at the base of her neck; with her
shining eyes, long lashes, and dark skin, she looked
like a young gypsy.

She shrugged her shoulders.

'He spat blood again last night.'

The postman watched the spaniels as they sniffed at
her ankles.

'Why d'you show so much of your legs?' said
Joigneau. 'Is it to tempt the passers-by? Or to give
the mosquitoes a good feed?'

She rearranged her legs, gave her skirt a twitch
over her bare knees, and said with a sneering laugh:

'What's that got to do with you, anyway?'

'That's enough sauce from you,' said Joigneau, leer-
ing. 'I'll be damned if you're wearing any knickers,
either. . . . It'd serve you right if you got a good slap
on your bottom, you little trollop!'

But she was already on her feet, and she jumped
nimbly to one side as she said:

'I'd like to see you try!'

The air around her was saturated with heat and vibrated as it vibrates round a camp-fire in the daytime.

The postman narrowed his eyes:

'If I ever catch you alone in the woods, my girl, you'll sing a different tune!'

He laughed, wiped his forehead, and went on his way – day-dreaming once more of the house, and the garden, and the vine. . . , It was the vine that stuck in his head most of all: a nice bit of ground it was, just right for the sun, and right next to his own strip. . . . Suddenly he slapped his thigh: 'La Mauriçotte – why didn't I think of that before!' He swerved across the road, righted himself, and pushed on, whistling.

He no longer felt the sun as it bored down on the back of his neck. The spaniels trotted behind him in the high plume of dust that hung in the air long after his passage. He was in open country now. Not a soul to be seen. Nothing to break the silence but the oiled whisper of the wheels and the two dogs panting. To the right, a newly harvested field lay open to the sun; to the left was nothing but beetroot, unrelieved by any tree. The voluminous roots, like teeth pulled free of their gums, seemed to hoist themselves clear of the dry earth in which they were stifling. A covey of partridges rose up with a sudden whirring, and as they darted off to the shade of the nearest hedge they flew as low as possible to save themselves effort.

*   *   *

Instead of keeping straight on to La Fourque, Joigneau
took a side path across the fields.

The Mauriçeau's cottage stood by itself in
the middle of the fields. As the two dogs came
up a woman of about thirty, dark-haired and
strongly built, turned round and looked across at
Joigneau. She'd been scouring a saucepan by the
well.

'Where is he?' Joigneau called. 'Can I see him?'
And more quietly: 'I'd like a word with you too,
Madame Mauriçotte.'

There was only one room, and it was full of smoke
and smelt sour. The dying man sat upright in an
alcove on a mattress of straw. He was propped up
with some old sacks of hay. There was no dresser and
there were no chairs. There was a bench, and an
up-ended box that served as a table; and in another
corner there was a straw mattress for the little gypsy
girl. Through the open window came the heavy smell
of liquid manure that has been dried in the sun. The
dogs toured the room, sniffed the nearly dead man
and went out of their own accord.

'No better?' the postman asked.

'Yes, I am,' said Mauriçeau in a voice that seemed
to echo among unseen rafters. And he looked at his
wife with a glance of defiance as he said: 'I'm getting
up tomorrow.'

Husband and wife exchanged venomous glances, as
if Joigneau had not been there.

'The only reason he wants to get up is to go and

get drunk,' said La Mauriçotte. 'But there's not a drop left in the house; and I know he'll never get to the village. He'd drop dead a dozen times over before he got there.'

Mauriçeau gave a hiccough and clenched his teeth. He was pinned down, helpless. The tables were turned now. Only six weeks ago he'd beaten his wife black and blue – for fun, not for any reason – and now it was she who had him at her mercy. He was strangled with rage: the rage of a wild beast in a trap.

*   *   *

They'd always been familiar figures in the region: foundlings, brought up at the public expense on the outskirts of Villegrande, they'd been married off to one another by the district inspector. She, serving in a local inn, had been got with child when she was seventeen. He, a poacher and odd job man, was feared and disliked. Often he was out of work; not many people cared to employ a foundling and a bastard. Necessity had forced him, before he fell ill, to accept the dirtiest and worst paid jobs. He consoled himself by spending his entire wages on drink at Bosse's each evening. When he was full and his pockets were empty Bosse threw him into the street. Mauriçeau would then find his way back to the cottage – tumbling into every ditch and scratching his face and hands in the hedge-rows. To appease his anger – or his sense of guilt – he then dragged his wife from her bed and began to beat her. And then, when he'd had his fill of that, another idea would strike him; and he'd lay her on her back on the mattress.

At such times her daughter would wake up with a start, and her teeth would chatter with fear and loathing. Often she'd taken her share of the beatings. And even, during the last few months, her share of the caresses as well. Her mother went back to bed and let him get on with it. At least there was peace, that way. 'You're not his daughter,' she'd say. 'If you were, I'd do him in.'

*   *   *

Joigneau kept to the centre of the path, with one hand on the handlebars. He took long strides as he explained the whole business. La Mauriçotte trotted along at his side and said nothing. In the end she said:

'It's too good to be true.'

'Don't be such a fool,' said Joigneau sharply. 'Leave it all to me. But there's got to be give and take, d'you see? If I find you the job with the Belgians, you've got to sign an agreement. The day you inherit from them, their vines belong to me.'

They'd come to the main road. She stood squarely in front of him, firm and strong in her wooden shoes. Her chemise had a dark stain beneath each armpit. The postman ran his eyes appreciatively across the broad hips and the big firm breasts. There'd have to be give and take. It was promising, all right: all that remained was to bring it off.

He called to his dogs, sniffed the warm air, and,

although there was not yet a cloud in the sky, he said:

'Feels like a storm. . . .'

*   *   *

As she went back along the path her thoughts were ablaze, and she could hardly walk straight, so intense were her hopes. What if he did call out in his last agonies? Let him cough out his lungs on his sackfuls of hay! If she could only finish him off and not lose any time. . . .

14

Madame Flamart's shop, with its notice VINS ET
LIQUEURS, was a low-built house that stood, in the
midst of the woods, at a point where three roads
met.

It was tight-shut. The postman parked his bicycle
in front of the window and tapped on the shutter:

'Madame Flamart!'

There was a barely perceptible scuffle within. And
then a voice, just slightly out of breath, cried:

'Coming!'

The key squeaked, and the door swung open:

'Ah, it's you, Monsieur Joigneau! Come in. . . . I've
only just got myself dressed.'

She wore a silk skirt, and the pink blouse which
she was buttoning across her ample bosom was cut
generously low.

The room was cool, and almost dark. There were
lingering, acidulous whiffs of lemonade and cheap
scent. Joigneau's ears were pricked; and he felt sure
that he heard someone gently close the back door,
which gave on to the wood.

'I'm not interrupting you?' he said.

She seemed not to hear him, as she took from the

counter a bottle of white wine and two glasses and came over to the table to sit with him.

He laid a letter before her, without a word.

'But it's for Flamart?'

'Never mind; you open it.'

She obeyed him. As she opened the envelope, the postman's eyes traversed her plump, bare, thigh-white arms, with their three disquieting vaccination marks; and then moved up, always with pleasure, towards the thick folds of the neck, the powdered cheeks, and the greased volutes of the chignon, with its mass of coloured pins and decorated combs. She was a fine piece of work, Madame Flamart, and no mistake.

She looked up and handed him the letter.

'I'd like to know who's the swine who sent that.'

He'd read it, of course, but he wasn't going to let on.

'Not signed, eh? I thought as much. Anyone with experience can smell an anonymous letter a mile away.' He adjusted his spectacles and pretended to read.

Suddenly the bare arm crashed down on the table.

'It's Cuffin!'

'You don't want to go accusing people without proof, Madame Flamart,' said Joigneau sententiously. 'And especially not someone who's taken an oath to his country.'

Her cheeks turned scarlet as she repeated:

'It's him! It's that policeman! I know damn well it's him!'

'In that case . . .' said Joigneau. He took up the letter again, gave it a careless glance or two, and smiled to himself:

'That old devil Cuffin!'

The village policeman was one of Joigneau's enemies. As an ex-company sergeant-major in the Territorials, he had a seat, in Bosse's café, at the old soldiers' table, where he often declared that France should have sacked Berlin first and signed the armistice afterwards. Joigneau suspected him of fomenting an underground campaign on behalf of Monsieur de Bielle, a retired cavalry officer who was standing against the mayor at the county elections. He kept a close watch on Cuffin. But what he really begrudged the constable was his uniform: he hated not being the only man in the village to wear a képi.

He slipped the letter into his pocket. He'd got something on Cuffin at last.

'Well, anyway,' he said. 'It might have made things awkward for you, if it hadn't been for me.'

'Awkward?' There was great arrogance in Madame Flamart's laugh. Suddenly she adopted a different and more intimate tone. 'Don't you worry about me – I can handle Flamart and his jealousy. It'd take more than the whole lot of you put together to turn Flamart against me. For good, I mean.' And then, almost at once, she was sorry that she had spoken so freely. 'But you were quite right to do what you did, Monsieur Joigneau. It would have made Flamart unhappy to

read that letter, and I'm grateful to you for sparing
him that.'

Joigneau rolled a cigarette, looked at Madame
Flamart from under his eyelids, as if he were nosing
her out, and decided to risk it:

'Just between you and me, Madame Flamart, why
d'you carry on like this?'

'Like what?'

When she lifted her head in that way, her nostrils
wide open and trembling reminded you of a first-class
heifer.

'Now come off it,' said Joigneau, all geniality now.
'You don't have to put on kid gloves with me. I'm
going to tell you just what I think, now the subject's
come up. To my way of thinking, a woman who can
go to bed every night with a big strong fellow like
Flamart – well, she ought to say to herself that she's
had her share. Yes, and she ought to let the rest go.'

'You think so?'

Madame Flamart wasn't annoyed. Somewhere on
her thick lips there was a smile, amused and discon-
certing: a smile that was not directed at anyone in
particular, but seemed to reflect some inward amuse-
ment. She squashed a fly on her strong white arm,
shook it on to the floor, and looked at Joigneau for a
moment before beginning to speak.

'I can speak openly to you, can't I, Monsieur
Joigneau? You're not someone who repeats things
to right and to left. . . . Well, I'll tell you something
interesting. Flamart's not a real man. That surprises

you, doesn't it? But it's true, what I tell you. Flamart's a big strong man, but he's never taken a woman in his life. We've slept in the same bed for six years, but he's never once touched me.'

She drank a little, put down her glass very gently, and went on, as if in thought:

'Maybe that's even why I've stayed with him, if you really want to know. I've had plenty of men and I don't deny it. People are what they are. But Flamart's different from the other's. I took to him the moment I saw him. A whole year he hung round me. Came to the bar every evening, sent me flowers and little presents. . . . But if I said to him "Come on up," he ran off like a little boy. In the end I got to know why he was so shy. You can't imagine, Monsieur Joigneau, you simply can't imagine what that did to me. I swore to myself that I'd give up everything and go and live with him; and I've done it, and I've never been sorry, either. I have to work hard to make a bit of money, but it's not for myself. I like money as much as anyone else, but what I do, I do for my man. I'm twelve years older than him. I may not look it, but it counts, you know. My sort of work's not going to go on for ever, is it? You've got to think ahead. And I want to feel that later on, even after I'm gone, Flamart will have a bit of butter on his bread, and a drop of cognac in his coffee, and enough tobacco in his pipe, and never have to go without to get it.'

She put her elbows on the table, took her double chin in her two hands, and looked Joigneau full in the face, not smiling, while he narrowed his eyes and said not a word.

'That's the size of it, you see. You don't want to judge other people too quickly, do you? Not before you know why they do as they do.'

'Well, I'm damned!' said Joigneau.

She'd quite taken the wind out of him.

15

The sky had clouded over during the quarter of an hour that Joigneau had been in the shop. The woods were like a Turkish bath; the mosquitoes formed up into thick clouds as if it were already the end of the afternoon; the scent of the mushrooms hung close to the ground. As Joigneau bicycled through the fir-plantation the red earth crackled beneath his tyres like frying breadcrumbs, and the tall bracken stood motionless on its slender stalks.

'Come on, Pic! Keep up, Mirabole!' Joigneau called to the two spaniels, who followed him with their tongues hanging out. Every few moments they flagged, only to get going again almost at once with a great noise of hard breathing.

Over towards Villegrande there were dark clouds above the horizon. And as Joigneau made his way back to the village, there were distant rumblings that presaged a storm.

Maupeyrou sweated it out. Its walls were almost red-hot, its shutters closed, its rooms airless and swarming with flies. The men of the village were busy from morning till night, with the vital, incompetent, age-old rhythms of country life. Untiring, with their brows creased from anxiety, they hurried to and fro, from counter to stable, from forge to coach-house, from storeroom to cellar, and from kitchen-garden to hayloft; and their women, with ant-like persistency, were busy in their turn, trotting from cradle to chicken-run and from stove to wash-tub, making ten pointless movements for every one that achieved something, and never devoting themselves to a coherent scheme of work – or treating themselves for that matter, to an hour of genuine leisure. They all bustled about as if locomotion were the main object of existence; as if there were not a moment to lose if they wanted to keep the last of all rendezvous; as if their daily bread were earned, literally, with the sweat of their brows.

*   *   *

Just as Joigneau was pedalling across the square, a gust of wind arose and swept the dust high up in the air – as high as the roof of the church. Shutters and doors rattled, the sky turned leaden, and the rumblings were more numerous and more distinct.

'Better light up, Ferdinand! It's going to turn nasty,' said Joigneau to the barber, who was inspecting the horizon from the threshold of his empty shop.

'Going to rain,' announced Madame Bosse as she trotted past.

*   *   *

In front of the post office, Joigneau ran into a big red-faced man, turning grey at the sides, with a black képi on his head, and boots; this was Cuffin, the constable.

Joigneau went straight to the point:

'What're you up to here, Captain? Hurry off – haven't you heard the news? Flamart's killed his wife!'

Cuffin stopped dead, cheeks as white as lard. There was a roll of thunder, and a long silence till Joigneau looked him square in the eyes and burst out laughing:

'Don't be a bloody fool, Cuffin. I'm only pulling your leg. . . . Anyway, you've told me what I wanted to know.'

He turned his back on the policeman, put the two contented spaniels back in their kennel, and buttoned his tunic. It was the moment for formal dress. Every morning, at the end of his round, he called in at the town hall to see Monsieur Arnaldon.

*　　*　　*

Beneath the bust that symbolised the Republic, the mayor strode to and fro in his study, with his pipe between his teeth. Monsieur Ennberg, just out of school, was finishing his report.

'Let's get this quite clear,' said the mayor. 'And I'm not going to mince my words. I shall never allow the Prefectoral authorities to bring pressure in that way upon the municipal representatives. . . . It's an insult to the principle of democratic suffrage. . . . I'll show them what I'm made of! We'll draft the letter tomorrow. And now let me sit in your place, my boy, and I'll sign those papers of yours.'

Arnaldon didn't waste his words. His conversation was always salted with such invigorating maxims as: 'Eyes on the target!' – 'Let's get our terms of reference quite clear!' – 'More action, and less talk, that's what I want' – energetic banalities which combined to suggest that Monsieur Arnaldon was a leader – a man who knew where he was going and meant to get there by the shortest route.

He was a man of nearly sixty, without a single grey hair. Regular features, cut in hard wood with a hatchet. Blue eyes, clear but not deep. A neat little moustache and a mouth like a letter-box. A face, altogether, that was stiff and dry: with the dryness of those for whom nothing has ever existed but their own will to get on.

The schoolmaster stood at the mayor's side and fed him with the papers, one by one. Each paper, when signed, was stamped with the town hall seal. Monsieur Ennberg found all this very discouraging. The ever-growing volume of administrative formalities was retarding, was it not, the proper evolution of society? A regime thus clogged with bureaucracy was a regime doomed to extinction. But of course he kept these thoughts to himself. He had long since taken the measure of Monsieur Arnaldon and his activities. He knew that for all his soldierly candour and manly loyalism, the mayor was not a man of action, but a garrulous old braggart – a man without method, or doctrine, or character, or integrity. Ennberg was compelled, as a part of his duties, to act as the mayor's private secretary. He kept silent, therefore; but he was ashamed of what he saw, and disgusted by what he had to do. It caused him real pain. He had kept, in spite of everything, the faith of a young militant. He believed with all his heart that there was such a thing as human dignity, and that in theory all citizens were equal and would find their salvation in the eventual triumph of secular democracy. He believed in the sovereignty of the people; and that men had the right to think as they pleased, to govern themselves as they wished, and to struggle unremittingly against an *ancien régime* that was always ready to be reborn under the democratic disguise of the capitalist parties. But these were, in point of fact, the principles to which Monsieur Arnaldon alluded over and over again in his speeches. That was what pained Monsieur Ennberg most of all; what he could never forgive the Arnaldons of France was that they were the derisory incarnation of a political ideal for which he, Ennberg, would gladly have given his life on the barricades of civil war.

Arnaldon had no idea of all this. Yet Joigneau, primed by his private censorship, had often warned him: 'You mark my words, Mr Mayor, that Ennberg of yours is as cold as a wet fish. And what's more – he's a two-faced fellow into the bargain.'

16

In the main square, huge drops of rain were plunging silently into the dust. The chestnut trees, dishevelled by the wind, abandoned their reddening leaves to the storm.

The postman was in a hurry to get home to his lunch.

La Mélie brought in the dish, and Joigneau sat down to eat.

He slumped in his chair, with his chin on a level with the plate, his face set, and his eyes half-closed beneath the undergrowth of lashes and eyebrows. He didn't speak. Unhurriedly and uninterruptedly, indifferent even to the squalls of rain which rattled his windows, he ate. And as he ate he thought of his intrigues. He was like one of the hairy spiders who lived in his attic, suspended for days on end in the centre of their webs, not moving, formidable, and ready to pounce at the first sight of their prey.

La Mélie was quite used to his silences. Joigneau the talker was known and admired for miles around; but Joigneau at home was a very different matter, and it was only to eat, drink, and snore that he ever opened his mouth within his own four walls. His wife, too, as she sat opposite him, was preoccupied with her own concerns; she picked at her food and had little appetite. Out of the corner of her eye she kept watch on her man, ready to pass him bread or wine at the appropriate moment; these attentions sprang from indifference – from instinct, in fact; conjugal service, nothing more.

There came a clap of thunder so violent that the whole room shook and the glasses danced on the sideboard.

La Mélie trembled, and broke the silence with a murmured:

'That can't have been far off. . . .'

But the storm was already over. The wind stopped suddenly; and with it, almost at once, the rain.

*   *   *

After drinking his coffee, and before leaving for the station, the postman went upstairs for his siesta. Rarely, however, did he actually lie down. It was the moment at which he boiled a little water on his spirit lamp; and then, secure from interruption, he would take the envelopes which interested him, and deftly open them with his big yellow-nailed fingers.

There was quite good sport, that day; notably a letter addressed to Cuffin, with definite proof, at last, of a betrayal which Joigneau had suspected for months. The mayor would be delighted.

But, in spite of this piece of good luck, the postman's mind was not at rest. As he sprawled across his bed and stared at the ceiling, certain images obsessed him. The little gypsy girl's calves, the sun-warmed hips of Madame Mauriçeau, and above all the lovely, thrice-vaccinated arms of Madame Flamart – all these had set him a-smoulder. He was like one of those live embers that lurk beneath the ash: a puff of wind would be enough. . . . There had nearly been a conflagration a few minutes earlier, when La Mélie, scarlet in the face from her meal, had come up to pour out his coffee. Her skirt had brushed Joigneau's knee. In a second he had put his arm round the great crupper – he knew it better than his own body – and pulled both wife and coffee-pot towards him. For all his roughness, La Mélie had known how to slip out of his grasp.

'You must be mad,' she told him. 'You nearly made me scald my hand.'

He laughed to see her so angry, and lapped up his coffee without a word.

*　　*　　*

At one o'clock, Joigneau put on his képi and set off to meet the 1.27.

It was the hottest moment of the day. The storm had been too short to do more than lay the dust. The air, though momentarily refreshed, was now once again at oven-heat. As he passed the cemetery, the blue granite soldier sparkled in the sunshine.

Joigneau got down from his bicycle and wiped his brow. Suddenly the mischievous embers burst into flame and took command of the postman as he stood, not moving, at the side of the road; for in the distance, at the far end of the track that led to the Bois-Laurent, he'd seen a red kerchief disappearing into the woods. That was Philiberte's kerchief; doubtless she was in search of firewood.

'Come on now!' said Joigneau to himself as he made off towards the station.

Duty came first.

17

From the moment he turned the corner at the foot of the embankment Joigneau could see the stationmaster pacing to and fro. The station hedge came barely up to his waist; and there was no mistaking his Quixotic silhouette and jutting profile; but this Quixote was old and bent and had nothing of the conqueror in him.

He called out to Joigneau:

'Nothing for me in this morning's post?'

'Yes, there is,' said Joigneau, quite shamelessly, as he parked his bicycle.

He was laughing behind his long moustaches. He knew quite well what the stationmaster had been expecting for the past fortnight. Joigneau had suspected the official yellow envelope with the faked handwriting from the moment he picked it out of the station letterbox. He'd thought it his duty to read it before it went off. And how right he was! He'd rarely had a more delightful surprise.

The stationmaster hurried over.

'Here you are,' said Joigneau. He took his time, and eventually brought out the Belgian stamp from his pocket.

'Nothing else?'

Disappointed, the old man looked down at the ground. It was a thing he often did; in fact it's a thing many people do; but the stationmaster's drooping nose, heavy eyelids, bent back and little beard all gave a particular emphasis to his downward glance.

'Soon be retiring, I suppose?' said Joigneau, to tease him. 'Not long to wait now, eh?'

The old man gave an evasive shrug of his shoulders, tucked the stamp under the ribbon of his cap, and went back to his den, with long strides.

*   *   *

Joigneau made straight for the lamp-room. Flamart was there, smoking a pipe and sweating away, while waiting for the 1.27.

'It's damned hot work on that road,' said Joigneau as he went in.

Flamart poured out a glass of wine by way of acknowledgement of this.

'You've seen her, have you? Did you speak to her?'

Joigneau wiped the back of his neck, sat down, and took the cool glass in his right hand. It felt delicious. He was thinking of what Madame Flamart had told him. The sight of the colossus amused him.

'Yes, I've seen her, and we had a chat. . . . You know, in a way, you can't blame her. . . . Not if you think things out.'

Flamart was blowing like a bull in the ring. His singlet was sticking to his body, and the great muscles of his breast rose and fell till he looked like an asthma-

tic fighting for breath. Suddenly he clenched his fists
and thrust his big face across the table:

'I'm not blaming her, you fool. . . . But that doesn't
make it any easier to think of the others!'

The two men looked at one another, for a time, in
silence. Then each withdrew into a detailed daydream.

'Money's money,' said Joigneau finally, by way of
summing-up.

*　　*　　*

Next door, in his office, the stationmaster closed the
booking-hatch, sat down, stretched his legs apart, and
stared at the floor.

Yes, in two months he'd be retired. Another
stationmaster would sit in his chair, and go through
the inventory, and take over the station. And where
would *he* have to go?

For thirty years he'd worn the company's uniform.
Thirty years, and never a reprimand; thirty years,
and not so much as a slip of the pen. Now he'd got to
retire. Like death, it was inevitable.

His career stretched behind him: the life of a stationmaster. It wasn't, perhaps, very grand; but he'd made
it flawless. For thirty years his only pleasure had been
that of doing his job well; and he'd rejected, with a
hero's constancy, those evil habits to which mankind
is prone to yield. He'd never smoked. He'd never
taken a mistress. He'd never even married. A man in
authority must prove himself inflexible; weakness has
no place in his life. The only pastimes which he allowed

D

himself were intellectual: his stamp-collection and his library. He was always ready to go through his album between two trains, or to browse in one of the fourteen calf-bound volumes which he'd been left by his god-father, an enthusiast for the theatre: Scribe's complete plays. All else had been sacrificed to the ideal: the perfect stationmaster. And now that he was on the point of leaving it all and burying himself alive, the satisfaction of having done his duty in no way solaced his despair.

The warning tinkle sounded. Train No. 209 was coming in. Luckily he still had his duties. But for them. . . .

He put on his cap and went out on to the platform. If only there had been something for him to do – some heavy traffic, a few passengers even! But the perfect stationmaster's platform was always empty.

*   *   *

Joigneau watched the stationmaster through the sooty windows of the lamp-room. A look of mischief flickered for a moment between his eyelids.

He was thinking of the advertisement which the old man had sent, a fortnight before, to the *Petit Journal:*

> Gent., midd. age, some savings, sm. pension, affect., sks. widow or y.w. Object: matr. Must be gd. hswf., affect., depend. Write Box 349. Urgent.

18

Joigneau went out of the station.

Why shouldn't he, after all? . . . With one foot still
on the pavement, he sat square on the saddle and
rolled himself a cigarette. As he kicked off on the
pedal he already saw himself in the Bois-Laurent.

*   *   *

Philiberte was a little black olive from the Midi. She
was thin, jumpy, shrill, and not really beautiful; but
with a goat's tingling activity. She clambered, bare-
legged, in espadrilles, over the countryside all summer
long; and even in the hottest weather she always wore
her red kerchief, brilliant and triangular, knotted
beneath her chin.

She was quite plainly a stranger in those parts.
She'd been brought to Maupeyrou by one of the village
boys who'd done his military service at Narbonne.
He'd died suddenly two years back; and ever since she
had lived in great poverty, with two tiny girls. She
couldn't go out as a daily servant, because of the two
children. She lived in a sort of mud hut on a piece of
waste land that belonged to the municipal authorities;
and she lived, more or less, by charity and looting. In

the afternoons she secured the babies in their cot and went out to gather wood.

Joigneau could always lay hands on her if he felt like it. As he plunged into the woods he whistled a hunting song. She never kept him waiting long. She followed him obediently, without so much as a smile of welcome, to the thickest part of the woods. He made her do things she didn't really like; but, if he chose, he could get the mayor to turn her out of her hut. Besides he always gave her a franc or two. They were quickly earned, and they bought two days' supply of bread. And it wouldn't go on for ever; as soon as the girls were bigger Philiberte could send them to school and go out as a laundress; it wasn't easy to get people who would wash, these days. In six months she'd have saved enough to get back to Roubagne, near Narbonne, where she had an invalid aunt; she dreamed of Roubagne every night as she dropped off to sleep. The people of Roubagne were very different, she knew, from the people of Maupeyrou.

*   *   *

From the top of the hill he'd seen them, all three of them, sitting between the willows by the water's edge: the three good-for-nothings, the three ex-service pensioners, 'our heroes', as the mayor called them in his speeches: Pascalon, Tulle, and Houstin.

Joigneau stood his bicycle against the side of the bridge and walked over in silence to join the three fishermen. Quarrel as they invariably did, they were none the less drawn together by some secret attraction: and you could always find them in the same corner of the square, at the same table in the café, and under the same tree at the water's edge.

*   *   *

Pascalon was lame – especially when he walked through the village. Of the three, he was the least lazy, the least obviously a pensioner. He was a cobbler and grave-digger by trade. Sent home in the first year of the war, he'd made the most of his position; on the very evening of the municipal reception which had been held for him at the town hall, he'd had himself appointed keeper of the cemetery, with a house – or rather, a tiny hut in the shadow of the churchyard pines – thrown in. He lived alone there; but his enemies, the three war widows, maintained that what went on in his hut at night was not at all funereal. Pascalon cared nothing for such gossip, and laughed it off. In the day-time, when the weather was not too hot and the lame hero felt in the mood for work, he installed himself in the shadow of the church and harked back to the trade by which he had once earned his living. A few shoes to be soled and heeled, a few clogs to patch – these paid for his escapades. Pascalon was a little man, with not a hair on his head, and two wicked eyes in his round pink face. If he was not to be found in the cemetery, or beside the church, he was usually in the café. There was no resisting him when he hobbled from table to table, winking and saying in his hoarse voice: 'G'd evening, chum. What about a drink?'

Tulle had lost an arm – the right one. It didn't stop him fishing, but it made it out of the question that he should work. His country and his sister – Madame Bosse, the café-proprietor's wife – looked after him. He lived in the café, got up at twelve in the morning, and studied the stock-markets. On Sundays he wore an apron and pretended to help serve the customers. His speciality was to take round the hat for the mechanical piano. He always took more than was needed to keep the thing going; and what was left over would keep him in tobacco for the rest of the week. As for the money he received from the government, that was sacred; he invested it.

The third pensioner, Houstin, had been gassed. He was the most envied of them all, because he still had his smallholding; and, over and above that, a tidy little pension as well. He was a big fair man, flabby and badly looked after, whose cheeks were never free from half-hearted stubble; he walked with hollowed chest and coughed a good deal – a habit (so the war widows said) contracted at the time when he had to appear once a month before a medical board. His wife, whom he'd left in the village, had gone off during the war and taken all their furniture with her. Houstin had come back to nothing but his house and Garibaldi, his dog: a yellowish spaniel whose hair, like his master's, could always do with a clip; he was a real circus dog, and brought in quite a bit of money when

Houstin put him through his tricks in the square in the evenings.

*　　　*　　　*

The meadows reeked of cool sticky mud. The river ran clear and fast between its reeds. The dark-green water took the long green grasses and combed them as if they were a head of fine hair.

'If only the fish . . .'

'Shut up,' Tulle said.

'. . . would bite like the mosquitoes,' Pascalon finished his sentence.

Houstin sat a little apart, propped up against the trunk of a willow. His instinct had led him to the only really dirty place – a point at which there was a bend in the river and the froth and scum had piled up into an oozing crust. It was in this filth that Houstin chose to cool his bare feet. He was half asleep. Luckily Garibaldi was sitting there too, to watch his master's float.

Joigneau stood and watched the river slip by. He didn't mind the cloud of mosquitoes which buzzed about his ears.

Pascalon turned towards him and smiled through a mouthful of ruined teeth.

'How about a drink?' he said.

19

Joigneau arrived in front of the mayor's house. From an open window on the first floor there came the sound of a minor scale: somebody was stumbling up the keyboard of a broken-backed piano and dropping the notes, one by one, into the street below.

Joigneau rang the bell at the outer gate. The scale stopped at once and Mademoiselle Arnaldon appeared at the window. Though hardly more than thirty she was already an old maid, and looked it. She smiled at the postman as if a surprise, of whatever kind, gave her pleasure.

'Good morning, Monsieur Joigneau. I'll come down.'

Monsieur Arnaldon, widowed early in his marriage, had remained single ever since. Marie-Jeanne was his second daughter, and the one who still lived with him.

The two sisters had always been members of what are called, in Maupeyrou, the 'fortunate few'. They had, indeed, never gone without.

In early youth they had been boarded out in Villegrande, and had there received the kind of education which lasts for a lifetime. Returning to Maupeyrou in the spring-time of adolescence, they sat down and waited for husbands. Their life, tranquil and secure, was supervised by Aunt Noémie, an elderly spinster who lived alone and independently in the other wing of the old house.

Year followed year, and the two young ladies had 'been out' for a considerable time when Thérèse, the elder, married one of her father's contemporaries, a rich farmer from Le Bourg-Eloi. He was a widower with an unmarried daughter. In marrying him, Thérèse was prompted by the fear – not that she ever admitted to it – of growing old, like her Aunt Noémie, with neither husband nor children to console her. Her life in the big farmhouse was envied and enviable: she drudged away from morning till night, with her elderly cross-patch of a husband and a jealous step-daughter who would never forgive her intrusion. People always need something to grumble at; and Thérèse always grieved that her husband was unquestionably too old to give her any children of her own.

Marie-Jeanne did not heed her sister's wise example. So far, indeed, from seeking a kindred happiness in marriage, she became more and more set in her ways. She had the busy selfishness of the complete old maid. Keeping house for her father, she moved passively towards middle age. The neighbours called her capricious and declared that she could never say 'no' to her whims. The piano, for instance: as a child she had always longed to study music, but even to strike a chord on the church harmonium would have compromised her father's political position. Therefore she made Monsieur Arnaldon buy her a piano which had slumbered for generations, beneath a double covering of cretonne and dust, in Madame Massot's drawing room. It was a venerable instrument, silent through a great part of its register, but endowed in the lowest octaves with the noble timbre of a Chinese gong. The old piano-tuner from Villegrande – he was blind, as tradition requires, and reputed to be a very gifted musician – had managed to restore to this piano the great majority of its notes; and he completed his good work by giving Marie-Jeanne fortnightly lessons. These visits to Villegrande were a delight to the old maid, who prepared herself for them with scale-practice and a liberal application of benzine to her gloves. So strongly emotional was her nature that she could never sleep the night before her lesson, and got up from bed with swollen eyes and cheeks even more blotchy than usual. But life would not be life without its excitements. . . . The neighbours were not mistaken: Marie-Jeanne, though a respectable woman, lived her pleasures intensely.

*   *   *

Arnaldon lived in only one of the rooms on his ground floor: the dining-room. There – when he was not hurrying round the countryside placating the electors – he could always be found. The table before him was never quite cleared, and his official papers kept company upon it with dirty plates, and butter dishes, and the bread-basket. Thin as he was, Arnaldon was the biggest eater in the parish – if not, indeed, in the whole county. He never went two hours without a bite. Ten times a day he would open the door and bellow up the stairs:

'Marie-Jeanne, I'm hungry!'

Marie-Jeanne was used to him; and down she would come with two poached eggs in a bowl of clear soup, or a plateful of cold meat, or simply a dish of goat cheese that had been brought to perfection in cinders.

But these were mere snacks. At proper meal-times the mayor reached his apotheosis. Even before the meal began, while his daughter was still laying the table, he took off the edge of his hunger by consuming, while standing up, a large pot of fat pâté. This he spread on slices of new bread, scouring the pot until no sliver remained to be scooped out with his wooden spoon. The amazing thing was that he thrived on it all. He didn't even get red in the face at the end of his meals. He got up when every dish was empty, drank a bowl of coffee and two glasses of brandy, lit his pipe, visited the lavatory, and returned to his work no more incommoded than if he had just eaten a lightly boiled egg.

*　　　*　　　*

When Joigneau came in, Monsieur Arnaldon put down his paper and looked up.

'Ah, Joigneau . . . you're just the man I want.' (The

mayor was a master of the simple, genial phrase.)
'You'd better get your things and come with me. The
police have had a letter alleging that old Pâqueux is
being kept a prisoner in his own house. The sergeant
tells me that they're going down to investigate any
moment now.'

'That'll be a joke,' said the postman, sitting down.

It was he who'd denounced the Pâqueux. But that
was nobody's business.

'And what about yourself, Joigneau? What's your
news?'

'Well . . .' The postman took a deep breath, just
to keep the mayor waiting. 'Well, you'll say I'm on
my hobby-horse, Mr Mayor. But you look out for
that constable. He's a lot too thick with your rival for
my liking.'

Monsieur Arnaldon shrugged his shoulders.

'Until you can bring me some proof . . .'

Joigneau took up the tobacco jar that lay on the
table and put it between his knees. He took his time
and rolled himself a *caporal fin* cigarette. Then he took
a piece of paper from his pocket and said:

'There's your proof.'

Monsieur Arnaldon read it over to himself:

Monsieur Cuffin, Police Constable
Maupeyrou.

Monsieur de Bielle wishes me to acknowledge
receipt of the confidential information contained in
your letter of the 22nd inst. This may prove of

great value to him in his electoral campaign, and he asks me to send you his thanks and most cordial greetings.

Yours faithfully,
Fabre,
Secretary to the Nationalist Committee.

Joigneau watched the mayor out of the corner of his eye and waited for a word of commendation. But Arnaldon was a real leader: he put the letter back on the table and spoke severly:

'That's not the letter you ought to have brought me, Joigneau. Cuffin's of the 22nd is the one we needed.'

Joigneau kept quite calm.

'Be patient, Mr Mayor. . . . I've got a friend in the other camp. He's on the job already.'

This time the mayor deigned to nod his head in approval.

Joigneau bent forward and stretched out his arm till his fingers touched the edge of the table.

'But that's not all, Mr Mayor. You ought to think of me a little. I'm not rich, you know.'

'Haven't you had enough money?'

'Enough! I've not had a centime since June. You've got to see things as they are, Mr Mayor. I don't care how much trouble I take – you can see that for yourself – and I think I can say that I put in a powerful lot of work in your interest. I've no time left for anything else, you know. Not so much as an hour a day in the garden. La Mélie has to buy everything we eat – even our vegetables. Life's dear, you know. I shall be right out of wine before long, and I'll have to buy a half-cask before the harvest. It's all got to be paid for. . . .'

The mayor watched him talking: with brows knit and drooping lower lip, he blew out his pipe-smoke in little puffs, as if it were soap-bubbles.

Joigneau played his last card:

'If I wanted to earn more I could get promotion any day in the week, just for the asking. I'm entitled to it. But I'll not leave Maupeyrou while I can live here and be useful to the party. All the same, some-one's got to help me. You've got to see things as they are, Mr Mayor.'

Monsieur Arnaldon said nothing. But he brought out his wallet, unfolded a banknote, and laid it on the oilcloth.

It was several seconds before Joigneau could stretch out his hand and say 'thank you'. It was silly, really: but when he set eyes on ready money the postman, so much the master of himself in every situation, would blush, and choke, and remain for a moment as if paralysed.

20

'Madame Sicagne!' Joigneau called out, 'here's news of that budding parson of yours!'

Augustin Sicagne was studying at the diocesan seminary.

Madame Sicagne pursed her lips and took the letter as if his words were an affront to her modesty.

The postman hurriedly changed his tack:

'He's got a fine handwriting, hasn't he? It's not often you see one like that.'

'No, indeed you don't!' said Madame Gueudet and Madame Touche, with one voice.

On every day that the good Lord gave them, Madame Gueudet and Madame Touche came over to Madame Sicagne's to work, morning and evening. They were the trio of war widows. They were more or less the same age, and each had a growing boy who was being educated at the Government's expense. Other bonds brought them together: their black clothes, their devotion to the Church, their love of gossip, the rancorous looks which they cast at all unwidowed wives, their loathing for 'the shirkers' (all men, that is to say, who had survived the war), their interest in the campaign for higher pensions, and the righteous chastity which, having withered and distorted their bodies, was now driving them quietly mad.

For nine or ten hours a day they toiled away at the stiff canvas bags which were then sold at an immense profit by a manufacturer in Villegrande. It was thankless work, which made their fingers bleed, inflamed their throats, and earned them just enough to keep alive; but it was *done at home.* So sought-after was work of this sort that it was only at the direct intervention of the mayor that they had secured it; and they trembled each week for fear that it should be taken from them.

*   *   *

Madame Touche was a heavily built woman, with cheeks like raw veal. She had matriculated, knew how to express herself with distinction, took pride in her knowledge of medicine, and was in great demand as an adviser on matters of health. She had found a job for her son in a chemist's shop in Villegrande, and he kept her supplied with ointments and herbal teas. No sooner did someone in the village fall ill than Madame Touche flew to the bedside – especially, so the gossips said, if it was a man's. The invalids would find themselves stripped, and prodded, and rubbed, and probed; poultices would be applied to their bellies; they would be cupped; leeches would feed on them; recalcitrant bladders would be sought out with Madame Touche's own hand. Her devotion was constant to the end – and often later: for she was always ready to watch over her patients in their last hours, and to sit in vigil over their dead bodies. She afflicted every young couple with advice that left nothing unsaid; be they fertile or childless, she kept an indiscreet and monthly watch upon them; and, where necessary, she would have certain catalogues addressed to herself in a plain envelope, little knowing that Joigneau had gone through them before they reached her.

Madame Gueudet, Leontine as she was called, was the youngest of the three. She seemed never to forget that she had been fair and pretty; she still kept her face out of the sun. Her eyes had pink shadows round them. She lived for her son, a pretentious weakly boy whom she had put in for a scholarship at Villegrande technical college. When he came home for his holidays he paraded about the village in his best clothes; his mother gave up her work in order to make the most of his presence; he was forbidden to go to the café with the other boys, and his mother went with him everywhere – even to the hairdresser. At Christmas he had had a bad attack of bronchitis; Madame Touche wanted to look after him, but his mother had never allowed her inside his room. Madame Touche took a cruel revenge. Incest, she declared, was at the bottom of Madame Gueudet's feelings for her son. Nor did Madame Gueudet conceal her own opinion – that Madame Touche had had the most sinister designs upon the boy's virtue.

*   *   *

The keystone of the trio was Madame Sicagne. Her name, combined with the length and thinness of her neck, had caused her to be nicknamed *La Cigogne:* the stork. Her melancholy features, with their encircling dark tresses, were held high before the world. She smelt atrociously of sweat. Since her son Augustin had been in the seminary a note of redoubled solemnity could be discerned in her. The line of her thin lips seemed to announce that, 'I have not smiled since I became a widow'. She had a dark complexion that gave her eyes an extreme pallor, and a look, too, of the clear water that lies still above hidden deeps. She had a gaze that pierced, quite suddenly: so much so, in fact, that there was not a man in the village, the Curé not excepted, who hadn't wondered at least once if Madame Sicagne were not in love with him. The joke of it was that she herself, in a roundabout way, was always accusing men of lusting after her; a man had only to raise his hat with particular courtesy for her to be convinced, and to put it about all over the village, that she had once again had to fend off a lewd proposal.

*   *   *

Madame Sicagne's tiny yard was, of course, a stronghold of the most pestilential reaction. But whenever Joigneau had occasion to set foot in it he sheathed his claws and lingered, if he could, in polite conversation: this nearly always yielded some ripe piece of gossip.

'They do say,' Madame Touche whispered, 'that

on high days and holidays she gets a lot of trollops like herself to come over from Villegrande and . . .'

'And help to keep her customers amused, I suppose!' said Madame Gueudet.

They were talking, as usual, about their neighbours. But Joigneau did not, for the moment, realise which neighbour was being discussed.

Madame Touche turned to him:

'Monsieur Joigneau could tell us a lot about her if he liked!'

'About who?'

'Madame Flamart.'

Madame Sicagne bared her gums in a savage grimace, and said very distinctly, without raising her eyes from the letter she was reading:

'Women like that should be whipped on the steps of the church, as they were in the olden days.'

'I'd do it gladly,' said Joigneau, with a laugh.

Three pairs of eyes turned on him like a firing squad.

From the street there came a diversion: the ominous clip-clop of three or four horsemen riding past.

'Sounds like the police,' said Joigneau, with the air of one who could say more, if he chose. He picked up his satchel and made haste to take his leave.

21

The policemen's horses were tethered in front of the town hall. The heat was too much for them, and they dozed in the shade of the chestnut trees.

The news had gone round the village like wildfire: 'They're going to arrest the Pâqueux.'

*   *   *

What went on inside the Moulin Blanc had long been a mystery. Even Joigneau had never managed to get inside the gate: the Pâqueux had two dogs which had been trained to give the alarm.

The property belonged to old Monsieur Pâqueux, who'd once been a well-known figure in Maupeyrou. During the war he lost his two elder sons on the field of battle, and then later his wife had died. There remained a son of twenty-seven or twenty-eight – the *Tonkinois*, people called him, or 'the Chink' – and a daughter, slightly younger. These two could often be seen in the distance as they worked in their fields. And often, too, there could be seen with them a child of four or five, who had come into the world, one winter's night, with none to witness his arrival. The *Tonkinois* had registered him as: 'Father unknown'. As for old Pâqueux, he'd not been seen for years. Nor,

until that evening, had anyone bothered about him.
But the muster of so many policemen had set the
whole village talking. The old man must have been
done to death: on that, all for the moment were
agreed. But what had been done with the body? Had
they buried it in a corner of one of their fields? Or
burnt it in their ancient furnace?

*   *   *

It was quite a procession.

The sergeant and his two men led off. Then came
the mayor and Monsieur Ennberg, accompanied by
the village constable and the postman. Then, at a
respectful distance, the men of the village, without
distinction of party – Houstin, Tulle and Pascalon,
Bosse and Quérolle, the Merlavignes and Ferdinand,
Pouillaude the wheelwright, and all the children from
school. Behind, as if at a funeral, came the women.
And last of all, at the very end of the procession, and
rather as if they were just out for a walk, came the
Curé's sister, Mademoiselle Verne, with Mademoiselle
Massot and La Célestine at her side.

No sooner had the policemen left the high road and
started on the track that led to the farm than the
Pâqueux's two dogs, which were tied up in the yard,
sprang out of their niche, rattled their chains, bared
their teeth to the gums and set up the very devil of a
row. Through the fence, the police could see the
heavy door of the farmhouse swing open, and then
swing shut again.

The procession halted. The sergeant, seemingly impassive, came forward alone to the gate and broke the silence with a cry of:

'Are you there, Pâqueux?'

The watchdogs, now foaming at the mouth, barked all the louder. If Houstin had not held tight to Garibaldi's collar, he would have rushed to the assistance of authority.

There was a pause.

Then there appeared on the threshold a weedy young man, with narrow eyes and low yellow forehead. The crowd set up a whisper of 'The *Tonkinois*. . . .'

He closed the door behind him, looked at the sergeant, and said, not moving an inch nearer:

'What d'you want?'

'Keep your dogs quiet and open the gate.'

There was energy in that voice: and a note of menace that struck into every heart. The *Tonkinois* fiddled for a moment with his moustache; and then, not hurrying, he did as he was told.

Nothing daunted, the mayor and his attendants followed the policemen into the yard. The rest of the crowd remained to gape through the fence.

'Does your father still live here?'

The man hesitated, and then spoke up quite firmly:

'That's nobody's business but ours.'

'I'm afraid it's my business too. I've got something to say to him.'

'Tell it to me, then. I'll pass it on.'

'I've got to speak to him personally, and to no one else.' The sergeant took another step towards the house, like a man who would stand no nonsense.

The *Tonkinois* stood squarely in front of the closed door, and said, looking straight at the sergeant:

'People can't walk into our house like that!'

The sergeant laid his hand on his revolver-holster. The crowd at once gave a murmur of disapproval: the Pâqueux were unpopular, but not half as unpopular as the police.

The sergeant took from his holster a sheet of paper and unfolded it in Pâqueux's face.

'You'd better look out, Pâqueux, or this thing'll go badly for you. You've been accused of keeping a defenceless old man under illegal restraint. We're here under orders to find out whether or not that is true. You'd better let me in, because if you don't . . .'

The two policemen made as if to seize Pâqueux and put the handcuffs on him. He looked at them like a hunted beast. Then he ran his gaze, quite slowly, over the policemen, mayor, and villagers. Finally he shrugged his shoulders and said, as if spitting the words from his mouth:

'Come in if you want to – I don't care!'

And he rapped sharply on the door and said, 'Open up!'

There was a noise of bolts, and the door swung open on its hinges.

The room within was a farmhouse living room, even darker and smokier than most.

Mademoiselle Pâqueux had withdrawn to the back of the room, where there was a bed and, above it, a boxwood crucifix. She was thin and slatternly. Her child, in its short little dress, hid its head in its mother's apron, so that nothing, could be seen of it but its scarlet bottom. The *Tonkinois* went over to his sister, as if to defend her.

'Well, all right,' said the sergeant, after a moment or two. 'And where's your father?'

'Where he belongs,' said the man.

'And where's that?'

'In his room.'

'Show me it.'

Son and daughter pointed, as one, towards a low door at the foot of the bed.

'You go first,' said the sergeant.

The man turned to his sister, and then went to the door and opened it. It gave on to a damp, dark wash-house; at the end of this was another door, which the *Tonkinois* unlocked himself.

The sergeant stooped in order to get into the tiny den, which measured about six feet by six. The smell was appalling.

The old man was sitting on a low pallet. His shirt was quite new, and seemed somehow to prop him upright. His gnarled hands had stiffened on his knees; and his narrowed, red-rimmed, expressionless eyes were fixed upon his visitors.

The room had a sloping roof: only at the entrance was it possible to stand upright. There was no ceiling.

A tiny skylight had been rigged up in the middle of the tiled roof. The floor was of earth. A clean bowl stood on a stool; and in front of the 'bed' was an empty slop-pail which smelt of ammonia.

'Good evening, Monsieur Pâqueux,' said the sergeant.

The old man, quite comatose, looked up but did not answer.

'What are you doing in a cupboard like this? Why aren't you in the front room with your children?'

'Because he likes it better here,' said the daughter roughly.

At this everyone, including her father, turned to her. She squinted, and this infirmity seemed to enhance the insolence of her manner.

'It's your father I'm speaking to. Let him answer for himself. . . . Why are you here, Monsieur Pâqueux, in this lovely weather? It's bad for you. Wouldn't you rather be out of doors?'

The old man looked at his daughter, and then at his son, and then at the sergeant. But he didn't say a word.

'Now come along,' said the sergeant. 'You must get up now. We're here to see that you get some fresh air. I've got an idea that you're not here of your own accord.'

The sergeant made as if to take Monsieur Pâqueux's arm, but the old man broke away with surprising vigour.

'No!'

The daughter gave a sneering laugh.

'You don't want to be helped? All right then. Get up by yourself and come into the front room. Then we'll have a little talk, just the two of us.'

'No!'

'And why not?'

There was a silence.

'Are you afraid of your children?'

'Not afraid of anyone,' the old man muttered.

'Then why d'you let them lock you up in here?'

'He's not locked up!' the daughter protested.

'You'll excuse me – but the door won't open without a key, and the keys of both doors only fit on the outside. That's what's called being locked up.'

'And if he likes it – what then?' said the daughter. She was really yelping now. 'Get the hell out of here and leave us alone!'

'Yes, get the hell out of here and leave us alone!' said the old man, in the same shrill tone.

'Now look here,' said the sergeant. 'It's quite clear to me that your children have shut you up in this hole so that they can run the farm instead of you. They've as good as stolen your property, and you are their prisoner. Anyone can see that, a mile off.'

'Bloody lies!' said the woman between her teeth.

The old man looked at her, and his lips mouthed the same words: 'Bloody lies!'

'Dad's old, you see,' said the *Tonkinois* with an air of sulky cunning. 'He's not strong any more. He doesn't know what he's doing. He likes it here. It's quiet, see? But he's not hungry, you can see that. He's got all he wants. Haven't you, Dad?'

'That's right.'

The daughter chipped in:

'Look at his nice warm socks. I made those. Dad's always cold in the legs, aren't you, Dad?'

'That's right.'

The son stepped forward:

'Show them your tobacco, Dad!'

The old man obediently searched underneath his mattress and drew out a filthy old blackened pipe and a twist of newspaper with some tobacco inside it.

The *Tonkinois* was winning now.

'You see, he's got everything he wants. We give him everything he asks for. Don't we, Dad?'

'That's right.'

The sergeant didn't know quite what to think.

'All the same,' he said vaguely, 'it's not usual, all this, you know.'

He bent down and put his hand on the old man's shoulder.

'Look here, Monsieur Pâqueux. For the last time: answer me the truth, now. We don't wish you any harm. Why are you here? Is it because you like it here? Or because they won't let you come out?'

The old man shrugged one shoulder, without a word.

His daughter burst out again:

'Whose business is that? Is he the master in his own house or isn't he?'

'Shut up!' said her brother.

Old Pâqueux shot a glance of loathing at his daughter. But he repeated, like a distant echo:

'Am I the master in my own house or aren't I?'

A silence.

The sergeant straightened up, shook his head, had an unspoken consultation with his men, the mayor, the village policeman and the postman; and backed towards the door:

'It's nothing to me, you know. I only came here to get you out of it. If you choose to die in this cesspit it's your business and nobody else's. Good evening, Monsieur Pâqueux.'

*   *   *

In the yard, a dozen or so nosey-parkers, more daring then the rest, were grouped in the sunshine in front of the door.

Mademoiselle Pâqueux burst out once again when she saw them.

'You ought to be ashamed of yourselves – bringing that mob here to hunt us down!' And she lifted her foot and grabbed hold of her clog, as if to bring it down on the sergeant's head. But her brother got hold of her wrist and she dropped the clog with a shriek of rage.

Outside they were beginning to make a joke of it all. High drama had turned to farce.

'Come on, now,' said the sergeant. 'Get moving there! No hanging about!'

He turned to Monsieur Arnaldon and said, for all to hear:

'You saw how things are, Mr Mayor. I've nothing more to say. You'll be getting my report.'

With his two men beside him, he walked with dignity out of the yard and through the crowd. People whistled and laughed as he passed; but he feigned not to hear them.

*　　*　　*

'Nasty sort of job . . .' Joigneau murmured as he gave the constable a violent dig in the ribs. 'Know what I think, Captain? I'd rather be a dirty dog of a village copper, like you, than a proper policeman.'

22

He made an odd sight at the side of the sunlit road –
the tall, stooping scarecrow of an old man who had
just come out of the shade of his garden. Monsieur de
Navières was undoubtedly the only inhabitant of
Maupeyrou who cared nothing either for the Pâqueux
or the police. He had more important things to do
that day.

As soon as he saw the postman in the distance he
began to wave his flabby old hand as if he were still
in the nursery.

'Good day, Paul. Do forgive me. . . .' (Monsieur de
Navières always addressed his neighbours by their
first names – and would have been hard put to it, in
fact, to call them by any other.) 'I wish you'd post a
letter for me. . . . In a little while, when you're on
your way back. . . . It'll need stamps. . . .'

'It'll be a pleasure.'

The old man, reassured, returned to his green
shade.

*   *   *

His was the oldest house in the village. It lay below
the road, in that marshy area which was called The

Island. It was a tiny villa, as derelict as its master, and overgrown, like him, with ivy in the midst of a virgin forest. It was like a chapel of rest in a long-disused cemetery.

The letter in question was addressed to the curator of the Musée Carnavalet, Paris.

'In the course,' Monsieur de Navières had written, 'of a life which has known many vicissitudes, a series of lucky accidents has enabled me to assemble a fine collection of miscellaneous antiquities. I do not wish these relics of the past to be scattered to the four winds when I myself am no longer here. I allude, Monsieur de Conservateur, to the four winds of the auction rooms. . . .'

The 'fine collection' consisted of a few yards of lace, a Bible that had been gnawed by rats, a flowered waistcoat dating from the reign of Louis-Philippe, two Roman coins that had been found not far from Maupeyrou, and a calf-bound breviary which Monsieur de Navières, as a result of his ill-directed researches, believed to have belonged to one of the canons of Soissons.

Since his retirement from the Bank he had given a great part of his life to these relics. They were kept in a cabinet of black pear-wood, in the inside of which he had stuck a notice addressed to the antiquarians of the future:

'This cabinet, with its distinction of style and attested authenticity, was constructed, at a date which we have not been able to ascertain exactly, in the workshops of Guillaumat, master-carpenter of Maupeyrou, at the instigation of my great-uncle Stanislas-Louis de Navières, who died in 1872. My uncle had been attached to the Ministry of Fine Arts, and had been able in this connection to render certain services to M. Garnier, the architect of the Paris Opera House. It may not be rash, therefore, to assume that the general plan of this cabinet may have been suggested to him by his illustrious friend.'

Monsieur de Navières was hard to date – harder even than his cabinet. His big limp body was ageless. He had fine startled grey eyes and semi-circular eyebrows, a fleshy nose, and a white beard. Winter and summer alike he wore a shirt of greyish flannel and a long threadbare jacket that was covered with spots and stains. He was alone in the world. He had been ruined by the war and lived in the recesses of his family home, with an old blind cat and a mass of small debts; she made quiet company, his cat, for she spent most of her time curled up on an old piece of cloth. Her only outings occurred more or less once every two days, when she went and made a mess in one of the corners of the 'library'. The 'library' (there were no books in it) was the ground floor room where Monsieur de Navières sat, waiting patiently for death, in the midst of an accumulation of dust-ridden bric-à-brac. Both the leaves outside and the ancient windows gave a green tinge to the light, till the room seemed more aquarium than library.

He was used to being alone, and had only the most

fleeting notion of his own decrepitude. He tried to rouse himself nearer to consciousness by talking to himself untiringly in a voice whose rolling r's had the effect, in the end, of sending him to sleep instead of keeping him awake. His strength ebbed with a discouraging slowness, although he had practically nothing to eat. He lived, like his cat, by dipping a little crumbled bread in his milk. His teeth had never been in good repair. Before the war he had bought himself a set of false teeth, but they had got out of shape and hurt his gums; and as he couldn't afford to have them repaired he had given up using them.

*　　*　　*

'Ah,' said Joigneau to himself. 'I'd nearly forgotten the old ruin.'

A zigzag footpath led through the nettles to Monsieur de Navières' pavilion. The door was shut. On the threshold was a can of milk, with a few small coins on the lid. It might have been an offering left there for all eternity in homage to some woodland deity.

Monsieur de Navières had no visitors. A ring at his bell always came to him as a serious shock. He got up with a jerk, stared around him in anguish, looked to see that his trousers were buttoned, and went off to open the door – trailing his slippers, as he did so, on the stone flags in the hall.

'Ah, there you are, Paul. Come in, my friend. . . . I want to entrust you with this envelope. Don't lose it,

E

now. It contains two copies of the description and inventory of my collections. "Bequeathed by the late Monsieur de Navières, member of the Archæological Society of Villegrande." If you happen to go to Paris, later on . . . I make some mention of . . . mmmm . . . but that doesn't matter. Here's the letter. Put it in your satchel. And here's the money for the stamp.'

His broad thick tongue thrashed about in his saliva with a noise like someone gargling. On the edge of his lower lip there was usually a large and syrupy bubble. That it would fall off seemed inevitable; but, deft as any conjuror, the old man always retrieved it.

'Right you are,' said Joigneau. Then, feeling the weight of the envelope, he said, 'But it's heavy, you know. You'll need another stamp.'

'Another?' The old man gazed blankly at the letter. 'Two stamps for one letter, Paul? You're sure?'

He felt in his pocket. Three small coins were found in his trousers, and another in the recesses of his jacket. Then he explored a cup that stood on the mantelpiece, one of the drawers in his commode, and the pockets of a waistcoat that hung in a cupboard. All in vain. There was, in point of fact, a banknote hidden beneath the cat's blanket; but that was for their next month's food, and not for anything in the world would he break into it now.

'Just a second, dear friend. I'll be with you in a minute.'

He'd suddenly remembered the money he'd put on the milk-can. La Mauricotte's daughter brought him a litre of goat's milk every evening. He paid for it in advance. Well, it couldn't be helped: he and the cat would have to make do with half a litre for once.

As Joigneau took the money and made for the door, the old man sat down and appeared to be pondering something.

'Ah, money, Paul! Money, money, money. . . . If I chose to sell my collections, mark you. . . . But I despise money. It's a thing that shouldn't exist. I know what money means. I was a cashier for twenty years. The money I've had through my hands! The bundles of it! The weight of gold! I've seen these things at close quarters. I've seen people come to my counter with such a look in their eyes. . . . Money, money, money. . . . It's the cause of everything. But there are people who've learnt that lesson. You know whom I'm referring to, don't you, Paul? I'm speaking of the Russians. You've read about it in the papers, I expect?'

Monsieur de Navières had no idea at all of what was going on in the world; but as the collapse of the Russian stock-market was at the bottom of his own distresses, he took a vague interest in the news from that quarter.

'They've abolished money there, you know. It doesn't exist. They all work, over there, but they don't get paid any more. . . .'

'Well, that wouldn't suit me at all,' said Joigneau with a laugh. 'Not at all, it wouldn't.'

'But why not? In Russia, you see, the state looks

after you. It's the state that gives you a house and buys the clothes for your back. It's the state that brings up your children. It's the state that looks after you when you're ill. It's the state that keeps you going when you're old. There's no more money. And no need of money, either. Interesting, isn't it? No more debts, no more creditors, no hunting for money for the milk, no more mortgages, no more going to law. . . . You don't have to buy anything. You've got it already. Of course it's not easy to see how it works. And yet why shouldn't it? Once you've got it all organised, why shouldn't it?'

'I like things better the way they are,' said Joigneau, edging his way into the hall.

The old man trailed after him. He was lost in thought. His eyes were quite vacant as he murmured to himself:

'No, no, things over here aren't so good as all that, you know, Paul. . . . Money's not a good thing, Paul. . . . It's something that should never have existed. So what's against it, my friend? Why shouldn't we change it, if it's not a good thing?'

He stood in the open door, with his eyes narrowed and his hand raised against the light. Staring down at the can of milk he took no notice of Joigneau as he walked away. There was a fixed, meaningless smile on his violet lips.

'The only thing is – it's not easy to understand. Take myself, for instance. I'm old now, and I'm tired. I'd like to be looked after. Someone's got to bring me my milk. Well, all right: the state brings it. But who is the state? The civil servants? Well, who among them? The tax-collector? The mayor? They've got other things to do. . . . And what if they don't think of my milk? What if they forget it? What if I just sit here and never get it? What then . . . ?'

23

When the town hall clock struck six, La Mélie put away her files, closed the iron shutters, and locked the front door of the post office.

Joigneau never came home till dinner-time. First came an hour's political talk in the café.

La Mélie had a look at the soup and went up into the attic. What was she after there? Did she even know herself? Perhaps she was going to see if her washing was dry. . . . It was the moment at which the apprentice came home from work to smarten himself up a little before going for his stroll in the square.

La Mélie waited for him. The attic smelt of damp linen, but also of hot tiles, lime-flowers, and mice.

When the street door banged, she called out to him:

'That you, Joseph? Bring me up a chair, would you?'

She came over to the edge of the trap. A puff of wind lifted the skirts of her summer dress. The apprentice looked up at that moment, on the landing, and went red.

La Mélie wanted to rehang the washing-line. But the chair wouldn't stand squarely on the sloping floor.

'Come on,' said Joseph, in a voice which was neither boy's nor man's, 'I'll hold you.'

She blushed in her turn – or thought she did.

'No, you get up. I'm afraid of falling.'

He did as she asked.

To reach the nail he had to stretch out his arms and tauten the muscles of his buttocks. His slender, powerful thighs were within an inch of her face. She could have stroked them with her cheeks, or with her fluttering lashes. The young body gave off a strong and healthy smell from its day's work. The blue overalls, stained with oil and grease, revealed the outline of the upper legs and the rounded thrust of the knee-cap. La Mélie looked down. His feet, in their brown espadrilles, were bare; she could see the veins beneath the chicken-white skin.

He jumped down.

'There you are!'

'Thanks!'

She moved away, sorry that it was so soon over.

Before leaving him she felt her washing and took down the stockings, which were already dry. She gave an unnatural laugh:

'It doesn't take long in this heat!'

He stood on the other side of the washing-line with his arms dangling at his sides, and watched her at her work. His big fat babyish lips were half open. He'd not yet begun to shave; but the light from the upper window gave his cheeks a little halo of down. The sweat lay on his chin like dew. He slipped his hand inside his shirt and scratched his armpit, like a monkey. He couldn't think of anything to say.

She walked past him, with her washing on her arm. As she went down the ladder, humming a tune, he followed her with his eyes.

Only when she was out of sight did he go into his garret. As he went, a pair of women's knickers, hung up on the line, brushed his cheek; he took no notice.

24

The day was nearly over.

On the square the trees cast all but invisible shadows that lay, pale and round, in the dust.

*   *   *

The evening meal was over, and Garibaldi was giving his evening performance in front of the café. He always had the same audience – the schoolchildren and a handful of older enthusiasts who never got tired of it.

The air had grown still in the heat of the day; but now it was on the move again, and it was pleasant to feel it pass across one's sweating brow.

Houstin made a gesture of pretended inspiration. 'I say, Garibaldi – what if we had a really good salad this evening?' The spaniel darted off, found a tuft of grass, dug it up, and dropped it at his master's feet. Houstin gave another order: 'Vinegar!' One paw was raised above the grass. 'Oil!' Garibaldi changed paws. Everyone laughed. And Houstin tore at his hair. 'Good God – you've forgotten the pepper and salt!' The dog turned round and scratched frantically at the earth with his hind legs till the tuft was buried in the sand. Everyone clapped, and the grown-ups threw down a few coins which Garibaldi picked up in his mouth and put into his master's pocket.

*   *   *

In front of the post office Joigneau and La Mélie were enjoying the fresh air on a bench with Joseph, the apprentice. It was the moment at which dilatory correspondents would come hurrying to the box with their letters; and often, too, a little group would form around the postman, and the talk would turn on municipal politics.

A band of young men, aged between eighteen and twenty, came out of the café. Before going home to bed they lingered to watch young Francis, the barber's son – the one who had 'no life in his scissors' – as he ran round the square. This he did every evening. He was a carrot-haired crafty-looking little fellow; dressed only in linen shorts, he tore round and round the square – and in doing so appeased, in some sort, his passionate appetite for action.

'Well, young fellows, how goes it?' said Joigneau, ever anxious to keep in with the electors of the future.

Among them there was a great strapping lad, the son of Joux, who farmed the Basses-Fosses; he was a hard-faced boy, already good at his job, who always had a cigarette hanging from his mouth, and walked with his hands in his pockets in an affected Parisian way. With them, too, was Nicolas Pouillaude, the wheelwright's son.

Joigneau wanted to tease them:

'Aren't there any more pretty girls in the village? You young fellows oughtn't to stick together all the time. You ought to leave that to us old 'uns.'

Young Joux had his answer ready:

'We're not like you married men, Monsieur Joigneau. We've got something else to think about.'

'There's a lot in that,' said La Mélie with evident approval.

'Well,' said Joigneau. 'He's got a tongue in his head, anyway, and he knows how to use it. But I'll tell you one thing, Joux. When you're master up at the Basses-Fosses I hope you'll be more accommodating than your father. D'you know he refused me a cartload of manure for my garden, the mean old devil?'

'You'll never see me at the Basses-Fosses,' said Joux.

'You don't mean to take it on?'

'No, Monsieur Joigneau. You won't catch me setting up as a farmer.'

'Well, I'm damned!' said Joigneau. 'What is it you want, then?'

'I don't mind what I do, so long as it's away from here. Don't you agree, Nicolas?'

Nicolas was no fool. He worked with Joseph in his father's shop, because the wheelwright would never agree to his taking an office job; but as soon as he was

called up for the army he meant to leave Maupeyrou –
for good. There was an edge on his voice as he said:

'We're young, you see. We want to see a bit of
life.'

'I suppose you think we know nothing about it,
eh?' said the postman.

'There's nothing personal about this, Monsieur
Joigneau,' said young Joux. 'It stands to reason:
everything's worn out here. . . . In the big towns
people aren't so behind the times.'

At that moment young Loutre jumped off his
bicycle just in front of the bench. His mother had sent
him with a basket of nectarines, still warm from the
sun, for Madame Joigneau. The wind had blown his
handsome fair hair all over the place, and dried the
sweat on his animated face, which was the colour of
the nectarines.

'So we're behind the times, are we?' said Joigneau,
as he turned to his wife. 'A commune in which ninety
per cent of the electorate vote to the left?'

Young Joux laughed:

'Yes, but we're not to the left, Monsieur Joigneau,
and we're not to the right either.'

'We don't give a damn for politics,' said Francis,
who spent most of the day reading the daily papers
in his father's shop.

Joux spat out his cigarette-end, took his hands out
of his pockets, and looked quite severely at Joigneau
as he said:

'Look, Monsieur Joigneau, you can see as straight

as we can. You're not going to tell us that there's no
room for a change and improvement in the world?
And I can tell you, if we ever do start taking a hand
in politics . . .'

Joigneau was quite annoyed.

'Impudent little devils!' he said. 'Hardly weaned as
yet, and you want to pull everything to pieces.'

'The old nuts are ripe now, aren't they?' said Joux.
'You've only got to shake the branch and see how
they come tumbling down.'

Nicolas laughed, too.

'You've not seen the end of it yet, Monsieur
Joigneau.'

Little Loutre leant on his handlebars. His cheeks
blazed as he listened, and his eyes shone. He felt like
a fine sailing-ship that's all ready for the sea.

Joseph too was transfigured. He got up abruptly
from the bench; his place was with Joux and Nicolas
and Francis, not with the Joigneaus. His life in the
wheelwright's shop suddenly seemed to him dis-
gusting and futile.

'I suppose you're on their side, too, Joseph?' said
La Mélie, with a nuance of distress. Her eyes never
left him. 'You're sick of Maupeyrou, too?'

'You bet I am!' said Joseph.

La Mélie hardly recognised his voice as it rang out
across the square.

25

Slowly the night drew near: it seemed in no hurry to take over the still limp village from which the day had lately fled. Life seemed to stand still in Maupey-rou; and everyone put off, from minute to minute, the moment at which he would return to his stifling room and get into the bed which, in every case, would be warm, and clinging, and all too narrow.

*   *   *

The 8.12 train had come and gone. The station had the whole night before it in which to sleep.

The stationmaster was up in his room. He had taken off, at long last, his cap, his stiff collar, and his cloth jacket. He sat down on the edge of his bed, unlaced his heavy boots and felt his sore feet, one after the other.

The last rays of the sun flared red through his window. What was the point of turning on the light? He had no wish to read that evening, or even to go through his album: he had already got the Belgian stamp which Joigneau had given him. And now that – instead of snatching a minute or two during official hours – he would soon be able to give the limitless leisure of his empty days to his collection he had lost almost all interest in stamps.

Below, the lamp-room was shut and sealed and delightfully stuffy; the ganger who took Flamart's place at night was snoring like a threshing-machine.

*   *   *

Down where there had once been a marsh the water-soaked countryside was already asleep. Shadow and coolness had triumphed, and the first star was shining through the poplars. Madame Loutre was coming back from the meadows with her bucket of milk. But her face remained hard and calculating; neither the softness of the evening, nor the sound of the accordeon which seemed to come out of the house to greet her, could change her expression; there is no time for repose in a life where only profits have any meaning.

Loutre and Fritz had finished their work. The little lorry was laden with baskets of melons, ready for despatch in the morning. Side by side, they took their ease on a bench made by Fritzy with his own hands. The Bavarian hummed a nostalgic little song and accompanied himself softly on the accordeon; he stretched out his white neck and held the accordeon next his heart as he drew from it the last fragrant notes of the refrain. His ear was alert; he cared for no audience but himself and the night. Loutre half spoke, half murmured the words of the songs; he heard them every day, but had no idea what they might mean.

Madame Loutre put down her bucket near the

bench and stood for a moment quite still, with her hands on her hips. There was nothing to suggest that she was listening to the sad little song. Around her, the smell of fresh milk mingled with the smells of warm earth and manure, and melons.

'Tomorrow,' she said, not speaking to anyone in particular, 'we'll have to start picking the peas.'

*   *   *

La Mauriçotte and her daughter sprawled on the bank beneath their hovel and were in no hurry to go back into the room where the consumptive was gasping for breath.

La Mauriçotte was thinking of the Belgians. If only the little brat didn't make a scandal and spoil everything!

'If you're really pregnant,' she said, 'the only thing is to let the Merlavignes run after you. Once that's done I'll make them take the responsibility. . . . But don't you ever dare tell what went on in this house, not even after he's dead – or if you do I'll get you sent to a home till you're twenty!'

The little gypsy listened as she lay on her back with her hands clasped under her neck. She thought with disgust of the two bearded bakers. And she thought, too, of Monsieur Joigneau, the postman. . . . She plunged her bare legs into the cool of the long grass and watched the star as it rose in the darkening sky.

*   *   *

As he lay on his filthy bed, sucking his empty pipe
and thinking of nothing, old Pâqueux looked up
through his flimsy skylight at that very same star.
Was it the star that winked, or his burning eyelids?
The smell of his slop-pail mingled with that of the
spoonful of soup that was turning sour in his basin.
Outside the owl hooted, as usual, and set off on its
nightly search for prey.

Through the wall the old man could hear the two
beings whom he loathed even more than he feared –
his son and daughter – as they thrashed restlessly
round and about in their big bed. In that same bed he
had slept for forty years, as the master of the Moulin
Blanc, with his wife beside him. In that bed, too, his
wife had died of rage and grief after the war had
taken two of her sons from her.

In the yard the two watchdogs, free now of their
chains, sniffed and snarled at the evening noises. Just
so did the three Pâqueux dream of revenge as they
harkened to every sound, with the rancour boiling in
their blood and the big farm all around them.

*   *   *

In the 'library' twilight began earlier than elsewhere.
It was the hour when the furniture could no longer be
distinguished from the walls; when only the looking-
glass still showed a small square of light; the hour
that Monsieur de Navières did not like.

The approach of night filled the old man with
watchful anxiety; he felt empty, and his emptiness

was like the giddiness that comes from great hunger; he wondered at such times if he had forgotten to drink his milk. His brain and his motionless limbs seemed to stir with the will to adventure; it was as if he wanted to see new things, to meet new people – better people, who were surely to be found somewhere. But at the same time – and he found this, if anything, consoling rather than painful – he felt himself incapable of any effort. It was too late. Everything was too late. And, what was more, it was really just as well.

For economy's sake he put off the moment at which he would light his little paraffin lamp. Often, in fact, he went to bed in the dark. Sometimes he even forgot to go to bed at all. Dawn would find him still in his old armchair, still talking to himself with his hands on his knees and his cat on the floor at his feet. His tongue never tired of rambling to and fro in his ever-watering mouth. Nor did he tire of his thoughts. He loved to think. He said as much and was proud of it. But he was so constituted that he could only think aloud.

'Money . . . Money . . . Money is the worst thing of all. It's a thing which shouldn't exist. It really shouldn't. Everyone wants it – the baker, the tax-collector, the postman with his stamps. . . . Nothing but money. . . . And no one's got any, that's the trouble. . . . In the old days things were different. But now, what with the world around us, what with politics – why, things aren't right at all, absolutely not at all. . . . So why shouldn't we have a change? Why shouldn't we alter things if they don't suit us as they are?'

He thought of all the milk that the state would bring him for nothing. He thought of the false teeth that the state would mend for him, without sending a bill. He'd be able to bite again! Why, he could bite into a crust of new bread and enjoy it! He laughed. It was delightful even to think of it. He swallowed his saliva, making a noise like a carp that's been thrown a piece of bread. Then everything became confused. Ashes fell on the village, on his house, on his own head. He dropped off for a few moments and woke up again. He was back at home. Everything was as usual. The cat was there. He felt quite well. He began thinking again: 'Money, my dear friend, money . . .'

He was happy.

26

The courtyard of the presbytery grew gradually darker. Over a cup of camomile tea, and under the ægis of St Anthony, Mademoiselle Verne, with the help of Mademoiselle Massot and Madame Sicagne, had just reconciled La Célestine with Madame Quérolle.

Upstairs in his room Monsieur le Curé gesticulated as he moved from bed to chimney-piece, and from table to prie-Dieu. His nervous tics now prevented him from remaining on his knees during his periods of meditation.

Madame Quérolle's shrill voice came up to him through the open casement window.

'If you knew the things he tells them in class, while he's supposed to be teaching them their botany!'

'It's a godless school!' said Mademoiselle Verne with a sigh.

La Célestine repeated in an ecstasy of horror:

'Yes! Quite godless!'

*   *   *

The priest strove to collect his thoughts. With his eyes on the ground, his arms crossed, and his chin well down on his chest, he began:

'O my Lord God, forgive me for my lack of courage.
I am stifling in this dry land. I know that not every
workman in the vineyard of the Master is called to
carry out the same task; that many among them will
never know the joys of the harvest; and that their
reward will be all the greater for their having waited
with confidence, and without complaint. . . . But I
cannot bear it here, and I cannot bring myself to
accept the task which You have assigned to me. I
ought to love my neighbour and yet I find in myself
more bitterness than love. Help me to love this godless people, this ungrateful race which has banished
You from its hearth, which has no longer any room
for You, either in its life or in its heart. They are
mad, one and all! They live as if it were they who are
eternal. They do not so much as glimpse the abyss
which waits for them at the end, nor how soon they
will reach it. I ought to be sorry for them, but I can
feel nothing but condemnation and hatred. Forgive
me, my God. . . . What right have I to be more severe
than You, who had pity upon them? And did not You
yourself say "Forgive them, for they know not what
they do"?'

*   *   *

The pious ladies continued their conversation in the
room below.

'I went there to buy some sorrel,' Mademoiselle
Massot was saying. 'And at midday they hadn't even
made the beds!'

Madame Sicagne went one further:

'I can see them from my window: and, do you
know, she's so lazy that it's her husband who gets up
in the morning and makes her coffee.'

'She's so vain, so extravagant,' said Madame
Quérolle. 'Every franc that her husband earns she
spends on her clothes.'

'She's not like her skinflint of a sister,' said
Madame Sicagne. '*She's* always dressed like a pauper.'

'Anyway,' said Mademoiselle Verne, 'when it
comes to gossip there's nothing to choose between
them. They're a regular pair of vipers – always saying
something nasty about someone.'

'Yes,' said La Célestine, 'a regular pair of vipers!'

*   *   *

The Curé floundered about his room. Suddenly he
knelt before his crucifix.

'O my God, what shall I answer when you call upon
me to give an account of my stewardship? How will
you forgive me the failure of my ministry, my parish
of infidels? Whose is the fault if the earth has proved
sterile? No doubt another and a worthier priest would
have brought it to fruition. If I had been more fer-
vent, more worthy of Your confidence and Your love,
I could have moved these mountains of impiety and
struck from these lifeless souls the spark which You
have hidden somewhere in the hearts of all Your
creatures! For is there not in all Your creatures the
reflection of Your divine nature?'

*   *   *

From the courtyard could be heard the sibilant tones of Mademoiselle Verne:

'The prophets have told us: that when carriages begin to move by themselves, and men to fly in the air, and women to live like men, this world shall be condemned and its end shall be near.'

*   *   *

The Curé got up, went over to the window that looked out on to the condemned world, and quietly closed it.

27

For a long time Monsieur Ennberg had given up his private studies. He no longer read for himself. His father-in-law, a chemist in Villegrande, had found him paid work with which to supplement his salary. Every evening till midnight the schoolmaster could be seen bent over his lamp. It was the only lamp left burning in the sleeping village. He was drafting brochures which served to publicise the medicines and fertilizers which the local laboratories had to offer.

But in summer-time he always came out, before settling to his work, and sat for a moment with his sister on the steps of his classroom.

In front of them the earth looked quite grey and the shadows of the chestnut trees had merged into the surrounding darkness. From time to time an early chestnut fell from its branch and broke open with a plop on the ground.

'They've broken another pane with their conkers,' said Monsieur Ennberg, almost in a whisper. (Every such repair, however small, involved a report, an estimate, and innumerable forms to be completed; he'd pay for the pane out of his own pocket before winter came.) 'And no sign of an inspector, as usual . . .' he went on after a pause. The school year would soon be over; and it would end, like its predecessors, in an atmosphere of general indifference, with no official observer to mark how hard they had striven and to give them a word of encouragement.

On the first floor, in the low-ceilinged room that was too small for the big bed and the cradle together, the children were whimpering. The heat had played on their nerves. Madame Ennberg pushed the elder girl to the window and ran the comb roughly through her tangled hair. The child was howling and stamping in her impatience to get it over. Her mother stood there in her camisole, with the sweat streaming down her face, and got her way with shouts, threats, and, at regular intervals, a good sound slap that made her feel better. The boy stayed back in the shadow, slyly paddling his two hands in the basin where his dirty linen had been put to soak. And in the cradle the youngest drew attention to itself by flying into a rage and beating the air with its tiny fists.

Mademoiselle Ennberg was even quieter than usual.

'And what is my little sister thinking?' her brother asked.

The schoolmistress gestured wearily.

'I had a visit from Madame Quérolle,' she said. 'What a woman! She said to me: "The girl knows too much already. It won't do her any good to learn more. We don't want her to end up as a postmistress. Or as a schoolmistress either for that matter." '

Monsieur Ennberg laughed his little nasal laugh.

The sound of an argument rose and died away in some distant courtyard. Then a footstep was heard on the road; and through the grille they could see the tall silhouette of the constable coming back from his rounds, with his cap on the side of his head and his big stick tucked under his arm.

'Yet I offered to take her for nothing,' Mademoiselle Ennberg went on.

She didn't say, though, how deeply she felt for the girl in question. For the first time in seven years she had recognised in one of her pupils a nature that was capable of generosity, a girl who had some ambition to instruct and better herself. Mademoiselle Ennberg had dreamed of taking her away from her sordid environment and forming and enriching her character. It would have rewarded her for seven years of almost entirely fruitless effort. . . . The tears came to her eyes at the thought. She wondered, that evening, if the sacrifice of her youth, her tenderness, her gifts as a mother, had been entirely in vain.

There was the squeak of a cart. Ennberg recognised the boy who was pulling it; it was Féju the road-mender's son. The schoolmaster waited for a smile or a glance from his pupil. But the boy went by whistling and didn't so much as look round at his school.

As if they had been thinking the same thought, Mademoiselle Ennberg said:

'D'you suppose that it's the same in every village in France?'

Monsieur Ennberg said nothing in reply, but he clicked his tongue repeatedly against the roof of his mouth. This was the signal that he gave in class when he wanted complete silence. There are some thoughts which must be deliberately set aside if a man does not wish to lose his courage.

Night had almost come.

For a few minutes more brother and sister sat side by side in the shadows. Occasionally there was a flash of light on the horizon.

'Summer lightning,' murmured Mademoiselle Ennberg.

The schoolmaster thought of his work, his pupils, and the morrow's dictation: so engrained in him was the instinct to concentrate on his duty and try to do it a little better each day.

His sister thought of her loneliness and of the life of the village, and of the animal quality in human nature. 'Why was the world so made? Was it really the fault of society?' And she was haunted by the question which she had so often asked herself: 'Or is it really the fault of Man himself?'

But there was in her so intense a longing to believe, such a store of ingenuous ardour, that she could never bring herself to doubt human nature. No, no! Never! If only the New Society could come to pass – better organised, less irrational, less unjust – then perhaps they would see what Man could do.

*   *   *

When the first stroke of nine rang out above their heads Monsieur Ennberg rose to his feet.

'Good night, my dear.'

She offered her forehead without a word. She had just remembered how badly she had slept the night before. And suddenly there came back to her the ridiculous nightmare which she had completely forgotten: her brother, in his shirt, bending over a bed and silently strangling his wife with the washing-line. . . .